FIRE
Six Writers *from* Angola, Mozambique, and Cape Verde

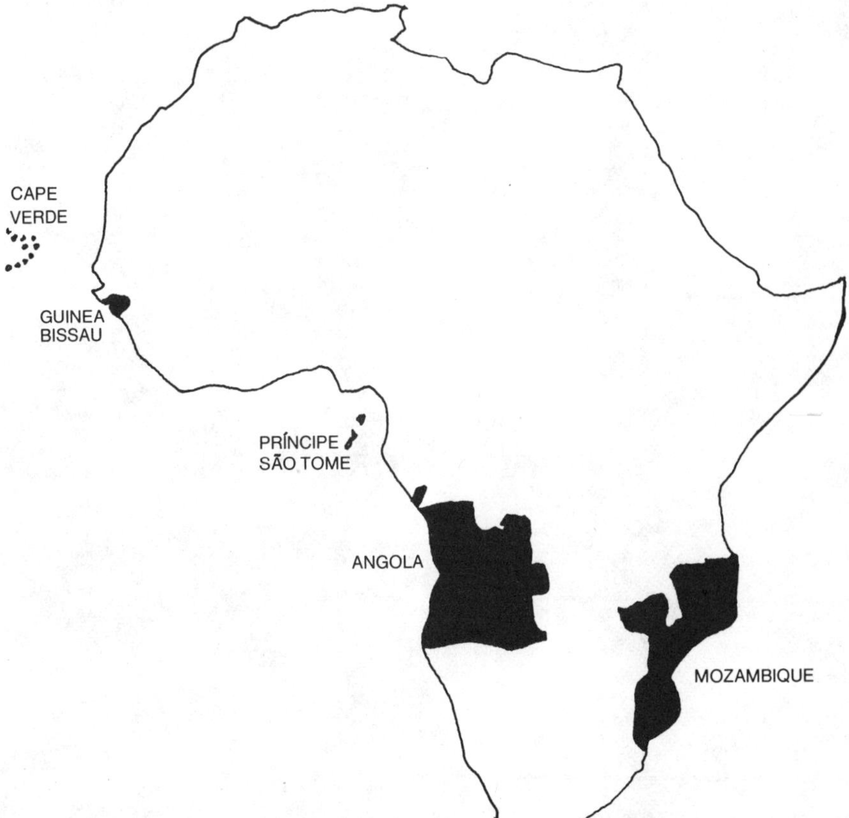

FIRE
Six Writers *from* Angola, Mozambique, and Cape Verde

by Donald Burness

With an afterword by Manuel Ferreira

Three Continents Press

Copyright © 1977 by Three Continents Press

ISBN 0-914478-51-6

ISBN 0-914478-52-4 (pbk)

LC 77-3840

All rights reserved. The reproduction in whole or in part, except for reviews, in any form or by electronic or other means, now known or hereafter invented, including photocopying, recording, xerography, and in any information storage and retrieval system, is forbidden without the written permission of the Publisher—Three Continents Press.

Cover Design by Inci Ankara

Photo portrait of author is by Ed Smith

Three Continents Press   1346 Connecticut Avenue, N.W.   Washington, D.C. 20036

FOR GERHARD

ACKNOWLEDGMENTS

I would like to express particular gratitude for the extensive help given me by Manuel Ferreira and Simeão Kafuxi. I am also indebted to the M.P.L.A., Arménio Ferreira, Luandino Vieira, Mário António and Geraldo Bessa Victor who provided me with valuable information, and to my publisher, Donald Herdeck, who encouraged me to write this book. To my wife Mary-Lou I owe thanks for her typing, critical comments and patience.

I also thank *Okike* and *Ba Shiru* for permitting me to quote from my translations which they originally published.

Acknowledgment is made to the following for permission to reprint from their works:

Geraldo Bessa Victor for quotations from *Cubata Abandonata, Mucanda, Monandengue* and *Sanzala sem Batuque*.

Livraria Sá da Costa Editora for quotations from *Sagrada Esperança* by Agostinho Neto.

Ba Shiru for republication of part of my article "The Short Stories of Geraldo Bessa Victor" in *vol. 6, no. 1.*

Dentro da minha alma canta e chora
   todo o grito dos muimbos africanos.
O fogo da queimada no capim
   é a febre que me avassala,

                Within my soul the echo
                   of African muimbos sings and cries.
                The fire of the burning in the grass
                   is the fever which overwhelms me,

                                 O Meu Coracão Batuca
                                     . . . Bessa Victor

CONTENTS

Introduction xi

Luandino Vieira and the World of the Musseque 1
Agostinho Neto and the Poetry of Combat 19
Geraldo Bessa Victor and the Voice of a Gentle Négritude 35
Mário António and the Face of Europe 55
Baltasar Lopes and the Morna of Cape Verde 75
Luís Bernardo Honwana and Lives of Humiliation 97
Eight Poems by Bessa Victor (translations by D. Burness) 107
Afterword by Manuel Ferreira 127
Selected Bibliography 137
Index 145

Photographs

Cover of *Chigubo* by José Craveirinha xv
Luandino Vieira 3
Musseque with skyscrapers in background, Luanda, Angola 5
Agostinho Neto 21
Geraldo Bessa Victor 37
Mário António 57
Modern Luanda along the sea 69
Baltasar Lopes 77
Cover of *Claridade* magazine 79
Cover of *Chiquinho* by Baltasar Lopes 83
Luís Bernardo Honwana 99

Map of Cape Verde 87

INTRODUCTION

Since Portuguese is only spoken as a principal language in two countries outside of Africa, Lusophone African writers have not enjoyed the same degree of international recognition as their Anglophone and Francophone counterparts. The Lusophone writer is an anomaly in Africa, for the use of a European language has not enabled him to reach a broad and variegated audience either within Africa or throughout the world. It is true that within Angola, Mozambique, Cape Verde, São Tomé and Príncipe, and to a much lesser extent Guiné-Bissau, Portuguese is the dominant literary vehicle, but the voices from these lands all too frequently are not heard by their African neighbors and others interested in African literature. In the first one hundred and fifty books in the *African Writers Series* published in London by Heinemann, only one is by a Lusophone writer. A few writers, among them Luandino Vieira and Agostinho Neto, have been translated into several foreign languages, but their good fortune is atypical.

To ignore the literature of African people who happened to be colonized by the Portuguese is to have an incomplete picture of neo-African literature. This literature does not merely echo the rhythms and themes of Anglophone and Francophone writing. Because of, and at times in spite of, the distinct quality of Portuguese colonial policy, an original and vibrant literature exists, particularly in Mozambique, Angola and Cape Verde. Much of this writing was banned under the fascist regimes of Salazar and Caetano, but the April 25th Revolution in Lisbon not only opened the door to political independence for the former colonies but also brought to light many books that previously could only be read by those who had access to unauthorized copies.

While most of sub-Saharan Africa was gaining independence in the early 1960's, Portugal refused to abandon her colonies. Consequently, much of the literature from Lusophone Africa during the past decade and a half has been a political literature of protest, and parallels can be drawn between this literature and the pre-independence négritude writing of Francophone and Anglophone Africa. Like their colleagues in Rhodesia and South Africa, modern Lusophone writers have expressed the frustrations and the determination of African people seeking to rid themselves of white foreign oppression that has denied them political and cultural liberties.

But Angola is not South Africa and Cape Verde is not Rhodesia. I do not wish to become too embroiled in a long-standing debate: the followers of Gilberto Freyre assert that Portugal was able to create a Lusitanian unity of culture and sentiment in Africa because of its Mediterranean temperament nourished by a long contact with Arab civilization centuries ago; Mário de Andrade in his celebrated essay "Cultura Negro-Africana e Assimilação," a preface to his *Antologia de Poesia Negra de Expressão Portuguesa*, argues that Freyre's position is invalid, that the Portuguese, like the French, practiced a policy of one-sided assimilation in which Africans were assimilated into a "superior" European culture. The high degree of illiteracy in Lusophone Africa as well as the economic exploitation do not indicate that the Portuguese were interested in a cultural synthesis. As is common when two extreme positions are presented, the truth lies somewhere in between. The Portuguese in Africa certainly were racists, but the nature of this racism is (or was) different from that practiced by the French and the English. Because many Portuguese who emigrated to the colonies were poor, they were obliged to live among African peoples in the suburbs of such cities as Luanda. Frequently mestiço or mulatto children were born as a result of this direct contact. Sometimes the mestiço was the product of a legal union; sometimes he or she was not. In time a very sizable mestiço population was created. In Cape Verde, for instance which is an altogether unique culture, over two thirds of the people are mestiço; in Angola and Mozambique the percentage is not at all large, but there are indeed many mestiços from these two lands.

Since the mestiço often has one black parent and one white parent, he generally grows up in a basically non-racist familial environment. Moreover, the poor white child growing up in a neighborhood with poor mestiço children and poor black children often loses whatever racist tendencies his parents may have. I am not claiming as Freyre does that a mestiço culture has resulted from a harmonious marriage between Europe and Africa throughout the Portuguese African colonies. I do believe, however, that as a result of the large mestiço population in Lusophone Africa, a unique situation was created and this situation is reflected in the literature.

In Andrade's anthology of "poesia negra" he includes António Jacinto, a white Angolan. Did Andrade not know that Jacinto is white? It would seem unlikely. António Jacinto in his poetry voices the conditions and the feelings of the Angolan people in a language that the people can understand. Andrade does not use "negra" to refer to color of skin (which is extra-literary anyway), but rather to refer to the content of the négritude poetry. Nor is António Jacinto an isolated phenomenon in Lusophone African literature. Gerald Moser's account that Senghor, upon reading Castro Soromenho believed him to be a black African writer, is not in the least surprising if one is familiar with Angolan literature.

Luandino Vieira, a white man born in Portugal but raised in Angola, is among the significant "African" literary voices to emerge from Lusophone Africa. I emphasize the "African" quality of his writing. What I am saying might sound like heresy or ignorance to those not familiar with Angolan society and literature. Let Luandino Vieira speak to the question:

> Literatura africana é a literatura dos povos dos países de Africa.
> Claro que um branco pode ser escritor africano. Há países africanos com parte da sua população de origem europeia. Essa população tem um background cultural diferente da história e cultura tradicionais dos povos negros africanos. Mas, desde há muito tempo que há uma vivência histórica comum, quer em oposição quer em concordância e isso faz com que as suas reacções nacionais sejam distintas por diversos factores que incluem também e obrigatoriamente, os backgrounds culturais. Uma cultura como uma literatura, nunca está feita, está sempre fazendo-se num espaço e num tempo históricamente determinadas e determinantes. Por isso, hoje, sou um escritor angolano, portanto um escritor africano.[7]

> African literature is the literature of the people of Africa.
> Certainly a white man can be an African writer. There are African countries in which part of the population is of European origin. That population has a cultural background different from the traditional history and culture of black African people. But, for a long time they have shared an historical coming together, either in opposition to one another or in harmony, and this results in their national reactions being distinct because of diverse factors which also include inevitably their cultural backgrounds. A culture, like a literature, is never static; it is always being remade in historically determined and determining space and time. For this reason, today, I am an Angolan writer, therefore an African writer.

Like António Jacinto, Luandino Vieira has been an active combatant in the struggle of the Angolan people to be free. While some black and mestiço Angolan "patriots," including Mário de Andrade and Manuel dos Santos Lima, chose to speak from the safe confines of comfortable Western capitals, Jacinto and Vieira were spending years in prison for their political activities. Along with another white Angolan writer, Costa Andrade, they are committed members of the M.P.L.A. (Popular Movement for the Liberation of Angola). Within their societies Jacinto, Vieira and Costa Andrade are considered dedicated Africans by their black "camaradas." In fact, Jacinto's poetry, which has been put to music, is as popular among the people as that of Agostinho Neto, the black president of the M.P.L.A. Because such a situation could not exist in South Africa does not mean that it does not exist in Angola. The fact is that race "per se" has little or nothing to do with Lusophone African literature.

To illustrate still further the degree of interracial commingling in Lusophone Africa it is interesting to note that the Mozambican négritude poet José Craveirinha and the Angolan poet Mário António, both mestiço, have written poems of affection and love for their white fathers, and when Mozambique became independent Samora Machel invited three white men to be in his cabinet.

Lusophone African writing also reflects the general Portuguese tendency to neglect those people who did not live in and around urban centers. Schools were not often established by the Portuguese in the interior, so that an African seeking an education had to go to Luanda or Nova Lisboa, Beira or Lourenço Marques to study. Furthermore, better paying jobs enticed those living in rural areas to move to the city. Since a written literature is the result of a "personal" contact between an artist and his environment, Lusophone African writing is predominantly an urban literature. Of course there are exceptions[2] but as a general rule the stories, novels and poems speak of life in and around the musseques of Luanda and the caniços of Lourenço Marques. Africans growing up in these communities were very quickly deprived of their own heritage to such an extent that many prominent writers including Agostinho Neto and Mário António do not speak the local language, Kimbundu. A Lusophone writer cannot, like Chinua Achebe of Nigeria who speaks Igbo, or Kofi Awoonor of Ghana who speaks Ewe, seek inspiration from firsthand contact with the oral traditions of his people simply because he lacks a direct knowledge of his literary past. Ironically, he must read accounts written in Portuguese of oral literatures gathered by European missionaries and scholars of earlier times—Heli Chatelian, Dr. Saturnino de Souza e Oliveira, Manuel Alves de Castro Francina, among others. Nevertheless, writers like Luís Bernardo Honwana of Mozambique, Baltasar Lopes of Cape Verde, and Luandino Vieira do not choose to write

Cover of *Chigubo* by José Craveirinha.

[Margin note top: is written/published in Crioulo]
[Margin note left: This is no longer true. Most "serious" poetry + fiction]

in the Portuguese language spoken in Lisbon or Coimbra. Although they cannot easily enrich the European language with linguistic patterns or proverbs or folk tales from an oral African past, they can, like the Brazilian Modernists, recreate the spoken dialects unique to each community. Unless one is intimately familiar with the odd marriage of Kimbundu-Portuguese spoken in the musseques, a book such as *No Antigamente na Vida* by Luandino cannot be completely understood even by an educated Portuguese who may have spent years in Africa but never lived in the musseques. A writer like Luandino, writing primarily for literate people in his own society, recreates the language spoken in that society.

The situation in Cape Verde is very different, for a bilingual society exists in which Crioulo can be considered as much a language in its own right as a dialect.[3]

The poets Eugénio Tavares and to a lesser extent Pedro Cardoso did succeed earlier in this century in establishing the possibility of an original Crioulo poetry which manifests in its rhythms and feelings the spirit of Cape Verde. To date, however, their accomplishments represent an isolated phenomenon, for recent attempts to use Crioulo as a literary vehicle reflect an insufficiency common to a literature that is in the process of creating its own roots. Most likely as António Aurélio Gonçalves asserts, Crioulo will be used more as a folkloric medium and Portuguese will continue to be used by a vast majority of serious Cape Verdean writers.[4] Their Portuguese will be the Portuguese of the islands, however, and the Crioulo influence will probably not be entirely lost.

The ethnic and cultural miscegenation in the Crioulo islands has no parallel in Africa. In fact, the visible absence of a sentiment of négritude caused Francisco Tenreiro and Mário de Andrade to exclude Cape Verdean writers from the first *Poesia Negra de Expressão Portuguesa* in 1953; Andrade does include such poets in his later anthology in 1959. And this is as it should be, for the regional character of Cape Verdean literature, its expression of *cabo-verdianidade* shares with the literature of Mozambique and Angola, as well as with Francophone and Anglophone African writing, a social and political posture that rejects the cultural dominance of Europe.

The six writers whom I discuss are all important figures in Lusophone African literature. Two of them, Neto and Honwana, are black; three—Mário António, Bessa Victor and Baltasar Lopes, are mestiço; Luandino Vieira is the only white writer I treat. All but Honwana have written both poetry and prose. I do not wish to suggest that these are the six best African writers in Portuguese (such a determination would be impossible), but each is undoubtedly a significant and unique voice. I have chosen one traditional négritude poet, Agostinho Neto, and consequently could not include a chapter on Jacinto or Francisco José Tenreiro of São Tomé, poets of great importance. I chose Luandino in preference to Castro

Soromenho because the latter has already been studied in some depth by Gerald Moser. Honwana and Baltasar Lopes are prominent figures in the literatures of Mozambique and Cape Verde. Mário António and Bessa Victor, Angolan writers and scholars who have lived many years in Europe, are included because of their originality and their artistic merit. To include only those writers who have been actively involved in their countries' social and political battles would reflect a one-sided picture of Lusophone African literature. Mário António is a complex writer, who in his early years was a spokesman against injustice, oppression and European cultural domination; but in time he has become more and more abstract, concerning himself with private expression rather than with voicing the feelings and goals of a communal African society. Geraldo Bessa Victor, a lyrical poet of harmony and brotherhood, is among the most gentle of all African poets. That Mário de Andrade chose to include Mário António and Bessa Victor alongside Neto, Jacinto and Marcelino dos Santos in his anthology is ample evidence that they are literary figures worthy of serious investigation.

Footnotes

1. Letter from Luandino Vieira to author, August, 1975.

2. The works of Castro Soromenho and Oscar Ribas of Angola, for instance, are concerned with African life in the interior. Soromenho's novel of the dissolution of a way of life with the arrival of European administrators and soldiers, *Terra Morta,* is set in Camaxilo, in Lunda, an area rich in diamonds. Historical fiction such as Manuel Pacavira's recent novel on Rainha Ginga, *Nzinga Mbandi,* does not reflect a modern urban environment.

3. Osório de Oliveira makes this point in his essay, "Uma Poesia Ignorada," as does Almerindo Lessa who, in July, 1956, organized in São Vicente a seminar on Cape Verdean culture.

4. "O Futuro do Português como Língua Literária em África," in *Colóquio,* no. 21. Sept., 1974.

LUANDINO VIEIRA AND THE WORLD OF THE MUSSEQUE

Luandino Vieira, a white Angolan, was born José Vieira Mateus de Graça in Lagoa do Furadouro, Portugal, on May 4, 1935. The son of a shoemaker and a country woman who emigrated to Angola to seek a better life, Luandino lived his childhood and adolescence in the musseques of Luanda-Braga, Ramalho, Kinaxixi and Makulusu—sharing with other poor whites, mulattoes and blacks a common lifestyle. He was able to overcome the racial prejudice of a colonialist society: "a convivência activa e mais tarde as leituras me fizeram libertar sempre desse estigma." (active sociability and later readings liberated me from that stigma.)[1] He went to school until the age of fifteen, after which he was obliged to work. He was employed as a dealer in automobile parts and as a service engineer for trucks and heavy machinery. At the age of twenty-six he was arrested for the disclosure, during a BBC interview, of secret certified lists of army deserters from the Portuguese Armed Services fighting in Angola. A military tribunal sentenced him to a fourteen year term, most of which was spent at the concentration camp of Tarrafal in Cape Verde with the poets António Jacinto and António Cardoso. Released in June of 1972 on the condition that he remain in Lisbon for five years, Vieira gained freedom with the overthrow of the Caetano government by the military on 25 April, 1974. Since that time he has been an active worker in the M.P.L.A., first in Lisbon and then in Luanda.

Most of Luandino's writing had been banned in Portugal before the dramatic change in government. Various stories and his first novel, *A Vida Verdadeira de Domingos Xavier* (The True Life of Domingos Xavier), had been printed abroad. At present we know of seven books by Luandino, two novels and five collections of short stories; he has written poetry as well. In general Vieira writes quickly; his second novel, *Nós, os do Makulusu* (We, the People of Makulusu), was composed in one week in April, 1967; many of his stories were completed in a day.

Like other intellectuals in the 1950's, Luandino Vieira became involved in a conscious struggle to effect not only the political independence of Angola, but also to create an Angolan literature that expressed the particular quality of Angolan life. The journals *Mensagem* and *Cultura* cried out "Let's discover Angola." Agostinho Neto, António Jacinto, Alda Lara, Mário António and Arnaldo Santos, along with Luandino, were inspired by the example of Brazilian Modernism. Jorge Amado, for instance, had broken away from a stale Parnassian literary world based in Lisbon to form a new and exciting independent Brazilian literature. These Angolan writers, like the French African intellectuals who founded *L'Etudiant Noir* in Paris in the thirties, were determined to assert their own particular African identity.

Luandino's contribution to the birth of a modern Angolan literature cannot be minimized. His early works of protest, set amidst the racial warfare that erupted in 1961 in northern Angola, speak of the dignity of the Angolan people and the brutality they endure. His tales of a ruthless colonial oppression, presented in a direct narrative style, are reminiscent of the pre-independence novels of Ferdinand Oyono of Cameroon. Luandino portrays the continuous assault on the integrity of an Angola victimized by ignorant and cruel Europeans who seek to preserve their domination, both political and economic, of a land that does not rightfully belong to them. With the publication of *Luuanda* in 1965, Vieira led a literary revolution—the traditional Portuguese language no longer served as a suitable vehicle for expressing the quality of Angolan life.

In an illuminating essay, "The Art of Luandino Vieira," Tomás Jacinto has made a valuable study of Luandino's linguistic originality.[2] Jacinto points out that Vieira not only uses Kimbundu words and expressions to create the rhythm of African speech, but that he also reproduces unique linguistic features that occur when Kimbundu and Portuguese are spoken in the same society. By dropping the "Ku" prefix of a Kimbundu verb and adding the "Ar" suffix of a Portuguese verb, a new verb is created, a hybrid verb that is conjugated as if it were a regular Portuguese verb. For instance, the Kimbundu verb "Kukambula"—to catch a moving object—becomes "Cambular." Vieira seeks to reproduce in a realistic manner the spoken Portuguese of Luanda. Many Kimbundu loan-words are consequently used. In his essay, Jacinto presents a list of all such words in *Luuanda* with their Kimbundu derivatives and their equivalent English and Portuguese meanings.

In his later works, Luandino also breaks away from a linear time sequence. He invents neologisms and creates linguistic patterns that serve his particular need. He is, in fact, through his innovations, revitalizing language, showing that the Portuguese of Camões or the Portuguese

Luandino Vieira

spoken in Lisbon and Coimbra, does not reflect the unique Luso-African speech of Luanda. Whether his characters are liberation fighters or impoverished dwellers of the musseques of Luanda, Luandino treats them with dignity. (His adopted name reveals his identity with the people of Luanda.) The lives of poor people matter. Their sorrows matter; their dreams matter; their joys matter. Like Jorge Amado, Vieira's love of his people is the source of his humanity. The poor folk may or may not be heroic, but they are never anti-heroic.

The fact that Luandino Vieira is white in no way diminishes the Africanness of his writing, for along with other white Angolans who have fought on the side of mulatto and black Africans, his voice and his spirit are rooted in the rivers, imbondeiros, capins and musseques of his land, "nesta, nossa terra de Angola." (this, our land of Angola).

A Vida Verdadeira de Domingos Xavier, written in 1961, was not published in Portugal until 1974. However, Présence Africaine published a French translation by Mário de Andrade and Chantal Tiberghien of Vieira's first novel in 1971. It is easy to see why the Portuguese authorities at the time were anxious to silence this Angolan voice that cried out against savage colonialist prison treatment and sang proudly of a strong and unified spirit among many Angolans who were willing to die in order that Angola be returned to the Angolans.

The central character in this novel, Domingos Xavier, is arrested in his village, his hands, feet and neck bound by a single rope. Brought to Luanda, he is beaten, kicked and starved by the authorities who ask him to betray two comrades, his friend Sousinha and his white boss, the engineer Silvester. Domingos Xavier does not talk. During their interrogation his body is a defenseless target of the brutality of the Portuguese authorities. But Domingos Xavier feels a joyful pride in the knowledge that he is able to be loyal to his friends and their cause. Perhaps the cruelest moment occurs when Domingos is offered a beer and sandwiches by his interrogator; but at the moment when he brings the bottle to his lips, a blow strikes his back, causing him to fall headfirst to the ground, his lips cut by the broken glass. Battered and bloody, seemingly without recognizable human form, Domingos Xavier's body is thrown into a cell with a group of nonpolitical prisoners. These motley men clean the blood that covers his body, cover him with a jacket. With an expression of peaceful satisfaction, Domingos Xavier dies, a martyr.

Luandino Vieira's novel, however, does not focus on a single character. Quite the contrary. Domingos Xavier's fate is most significant in that it brings together many Angolans who are engaged in a common struggle of liberation. There is the tailor, Mussunda, an intellectual who helps direct the activities of the underground. Mussunda is a socialist who refuses to see the Angolan situation in terms of white, black and

Musseque with skyscrapers in background, Luanda, Angola.

mulatto. There are only two factions: the rich and the poor, who work so that the rich can become richer. Mussunda echoes the sentiments expressed by James Ngugi in his book of essays, *Homecoming*, in which Ngugi asserts that Africa in our time has only two tribes: the haves and the have nots. Mussunda has converted Chico João to the cause. Chico João, a football player, a ladies' man, lives a life of irrelevant details until at the age of twenty-four, he realizes that life is serious business and that as an Angolan he, like many others, has serious responsibilities if his country is to free itself from the greedy clutches of Portugal. Zito, a boy trained to perceive any irregularity in the conduct of the police, and his grandfather, the old man Petolo, constitute an important element in the popular movement. It is Zito who reports to his grandfather that an unidentified activist has been taken into custody by the colonialist authorities. Petolo reports to Chico João who in turn informs Mussunda of this sad event. The tailor sends out a comrade, Miguel, who learns the identity of the prisoner. There is a distinct hierarchy among the militants of the clandestine nationalist organization. Each member accepts his particular responsibilities.

Nearly all who occupy privileged positions maintain their status through a constant oppression of the Angolan masses. The white prison administrators, the whites who ride the bus and insult black passengers, the blacks Mandombe and João who beat Domingos with a special whip called a "palmatoria"—these people are motivated purely by greed and power. But there are exceptions. Mr. Silvester is completely sympathetic to the goals of the liberation movement. He has learned Kimbundu; he does not possess the colonialist mentality which denigrates everything that is not European. In fact, he is on intimate terms with various members of the struggle. His workers eat their traditional food rather than Portuguese food which they do not like. He recognizes the injustice of the colonial system and fights to effect a new social situation. He is a "mano," a brother (popular form for irmão), a compatriot and a comrade of the black Angolan people. It is of significance that Mussunda, in announcing to the people that Domingos Xavier is dead, first addresses them as "African compatriots" and then, seeing Silvester, realizes his mistake and speaks to the "Angolan compatriots". For Vieira, the question of race is supererogatory; an Angolan is he who lives and dies for Angola. Angola is for Angolans, not merely black Africans of Angola.[3]

Angola itself is perhaps the dominant figure in the novel. The river Kuanza runs at times fiercely, at times gently, through the minds of several characters. Domingos Xavier, the tractor driver, follows the Kuanza from its sources to the ocean the day of his death. The moon of Angola, the rain, the musseques, the huts, the plains, the hills, the stars—they appear and reappear, for they are as much a part of Angola as Domingos and his friends. In a very tender passage, Vieira recounts that the dead

Domingos resides far away in the moonlight of Angola, which will, every night, tell his story. But this is not merely a poetic metaphor or clever fable; it is essential to the novel to see the Angolan landscape as a synedoche for Angola itself; man and nature constitute the country. *A Vida Verdadeira de Domingos Xavier* ends with celebration. The "Festa de Bairro Operário", filled with music and dancing, must go on, for as Mussunda tells his colleagues, such an expression of the vitality of the people, a celebration of life itself, is the necessary tribute to the courage of prisoners like Domingos Xavier and Liceu (an actual historical figure), the artist-militant-troubador of his generation. This note of triumph, like the fate of Domingos Xavier, serves to bring the community together in an assertion of its identity, its values and its will to survive.

A Vida Verdadeira de Domingos Xavier is one of a numerous collection of African literary works which are concerned with prison life. In South African literature, Robben Island, the notorious political camp, is the subject of several works. Dennis Brutus wrote a series of poems, *Letters to Martha,* describing his experiences as a prisoner. Z.M. Zwelonke's novel, *Robben Island,* and Athol Fugard's play, *The Island,* also depict with horrible realism the barbarousness of prison life. Vieira, as a competent artist, has not merely written a novel about an Angolan prison. It is common knowledge that political prisons from the Gulag Archipelago to Dachau are awful places where day to day life is a struggle against overt physical and psychological torture. But prison experience does not easily lend itself to good literature, for the writer must go beyond the obvious fact that political prisons are not admirable institutions. Vieira's triumph lies in his creating individual characters whose lives matter. In his novel, the suffering of Domingos' wife Maria and his child Bastião makes us feel the value of this man. He is not merely a political activist; he is a man who loves the earth and sky and water and his family, and he in turn is loved by them. Moreover, the conclusion of the novel points to a future in which Angola will be free to construct her own destiny, and affirms that a human life given in a just cause is a cause for celebration not despair.

* * * *

The eight short stories comprising Vieira's third book were written between June 28 and July 28, 1962 while he was in the PIDE[4] detention center, the Pavilhão Prisional, in Luanda. *Vidas Novas* (New Lives) has had various clandestine editions, not all of them complete. Edições Anti-Colonial first published the stories in an undated edition which appeared in Paris. The first legal edition that Vieira himself has been able to read was published in April, 1975, by Afrontamento. *Vidas Novas* was awarded the João Dias prize in 1962 by the Casa dos Estudantes do Império in Lisbon by a jury that included among others Noémia de Sousa, Carlos Ervedosa, Urbana Tavares Rodrigues, Orlando da Costa and Lília da Fonseca.

Rain beats down on the lives of the people of *Vidas Novas* with an ineluctable force that reminds one of the ubiquitous patrol vans, jeeps, machine guns and sirens that continually threaten the lives of the residents of the musseques. The tales are stories of protest against oppression, brutality, injustice and racism. Moreover, they assert the pride of the committed Angolan willing to die for freedom, a pride which overcomes the sense of shame and inadequacy that has been bred by Portuguese colonial policies. Read in succession the stories are monotonous. The same basic plot is apparent throughout. The dedicated fighter for Angola or the newly converted combatant faces insults, torture, and in two stories, death itself, in order to further the liberation struggle of the Angolan people. Children, young men and women, and older people alike willingly sacrifice the calm of noncommitment for a cause they consider to be worth whatever pain they must endure. Whereas in the novel, *A Vida Verdadeira de Domingos Xavier,* Vieira has sufficient space to create individual characters with distinct qualities and values, in *Vidas Novas* he only succeeds in creating a pantheon of heroic figures who can inspire the people of Angola by their bravery and dedication. The plots become mechanical. After reading several stories, the reader can predict what will happen to the remaining characters and how they will react. Characterization is sacrificed to political statement. Consequently these stories, more often than not, are hollow reproductions.

Two of these stories, however, are of particular interest because they go beyond a mere realistic portrayal of the liberation struggle. "O Fato Completo de Lucas Matesso" through humor and irony shows the ignorance of white Portuguese civil servants of African customs and values. These officials manifest the same cultural arrogance of Europe as Chinua Achebe's District Commissioner who at the end of *Things Fall Apart* confidently plans to write a study, *The Pacification of the Primitive Tribes of the Lower Niger,* on the Igbo people about whom he has neither understanding nor appreciation; on the contrary, he continually interprets African customs from a myopic Western vantage point and views Africans as primitive and backward. In "O Fato Completo de Lucas Matesso" Chefe Reis and Artur the prison guard brutally beat, kick, punish and even starve the prisoner Lucas Matesso, demanding that he tell them the secret of the "fato completo" that they have learned will be sent him by his wife, Maria. "Fato completo" in Portuguese means "a suit"; naturally Chefe Reis is frustrated and confounded when on visiting day the prisoner's wife does not bring the expected garment, for he has assumed that a message will be hidden in the lining or the pockets. He goes so far as to rip apart the pajamas that are brought, thinking that perhaps this article of clothing has been substituted for the anticipated suit. But to his consternation, he can find no valuable information. It is at the conclusion of the story that we realize that for the people of the musseque, "fato completo" is the name of a particularly delicious meal made of palm oil, green beans, fish and bananas wrapped in paper. Earlier in the story, Reis had commented on the inedible food of Africans. More than likely he had never tasted it. Reis is a contrast to Mr. Silvester in *A Vida Verdadeira de Domingos Xavier*, who not only speaks Kimbundu but recognizes that the Africans prefer their own food. Reis' confusion is a direct result of his ignorance. The story concludes with Lucas Matesso laughing aloud at the irony of the situation and looking forward to eating his "fato completo."

Like Domingas Xavier, Lucas Matesso takes refuge in memories of the rivers of his land:

> E era o Lukala que ele via, o rio da terra mijando a água boa nas lavros. O Lukalo descendo, vagaroso e seguro, sem medo, já depois do salto do Duque de Bragança, a correr para se deitar em cima das águas do mais—velho Kuanza e, de mão dada, seguirem os dois na direcção do mar.
> Essa figura assim, das águas do rio e dos capins dos lados a dançar no vento, os dendens pendurados nas palmeiras, as lavras verdes de milho e mandioca, deram berrida nas dores, não sentia mais o chicote outra vez a bater . . .[5]

And it was the Lukala that he was seeing, the river of his homeland spilling good water onto the tilled earth. The Lukala, descending slowly and surely, without fear, already beyond the Duke of Bragança Falls, running in order to join the waters of the older Kuanza, hand-in-hand, as they go on together in the direction of the sea.

Thus images of the waters of the river and the high grass on the banks dancing in the wind, the denden fruit hung from the palm trees, the soil green with corn and manioc, assuaged his pains, he no longer felt the whip beating him again. . .

It is in such passages that we feel Vieira's love of the Angolan landscape, an assertion of the enduring beauty of his country.

"O Fato Completo de Lucas Matesso" has been published in the Algerian journal *Novembre* (no. 4, 1965) and in France, first in *France Nouvelle* and later in conjunction with *A Vida Verdadeira de Domingos Xavier* by Présence Africaine. It is easy to see why this particular story has been set apart from the others in *Vidas Novas*.

In "O Feitiço no Bufo Toneto" (The Bewitching of the Spy Toneto)

Luandino Vieira returns to the traditional African world of magic and witchcraft, even though the story is a modern political tale of activism and betrayal in Angola in the early 1960's. João Santos, a mulatto just released from prison, the intellectual Estudante, and Kakuiji, an auto repair worker, plot to punish Toneto Gomes because they are sure that it is he who is betraying them to the PIDE. In a serious debate in which Kakuiji opts for murdering the traitor, João and Estudante feel that such action would be self-defeating, since the killer would have to face a long prison sentence. It is finally determined that he should be punished by witchcraft. Estudante, the mastermind behind the plot, thinks of witchcraft as "essas histórias de monandengues" (these stories of childhood). He believes that in the past the witchdoctor often used his putative power merely to deceive the people into paying him. The traditional African sorcerer frequently was nothing but a thief who took advantage of particular situations to gain wealth and seduce women. João Santos thinks the scheme a clever game while Kakuiji, though somewhat afraid, is willing to go along with the ruse. In fact, it is he who is selected to be the "witchdoctor" on the fatal night. Once the plan has been determined, Estudante becomes more and more dubious. However, remembering a story of long ago, told by o velho Kamukata, of a witch-doctor who made weird sounds resembling a goat, he encourages Kakuiji to make similar sounds audible only to Toneto Gomes. Dressed in a traditional costume, Kakuiji gets carried away. At the home of Toneto he bellows the sound of the goat so that the whole community is awakened. Kakuiji has bewitched himself into believing he is an actual witchdoctor, an incarnation from Africa's past.

He puts himself into a trance. João and Estudante have to forcibly remove him from the scene. Poor Toneto Gomes is so upset by the curse that he goes insane. He believes that his spirit being has been taken away from him. We later learn that the family of Kakuiji was reportedly killed by witchcraft and the people believe that he has received magic powers in order to punish others. Toneto's boss, Chefe Costa, refuses to heed his demand that since the witchdoctor is an enemy of the state, he should be incarcerated. Betrayed by the white man who has always accepted his complaints about revolutionaries in the past, Toneto Gomes runs through the streets screaming that he is not a PIDE. What has started as a joke has turned out to be an effective means of punishing the traitor.

By going back to Africa's past, Vieira illustrates that the African psyche is not a reproduction of Western rationalism. The vitality of "O Feitiço no Bufo Toneto" stems from the author's use of traditional wisdom to solve a modern problem. Oscar Ribas, another Angolan writer, also uses the theme of witchcraft in his story "A Praga" (The Curse). The return to a purely African past in specific Angolan stories is ample evidence that writers such as Vieira and Ribas are not content to see African literature as an extension of Portuguese literature, but rather as an expression of the values and essence of an African way of life.

* * * *

The awarding by the Sociedade Portuguesa de Escritores of its highest prize to Luandino Vieira in 1965 for *Luuanda* caused an uproar. The fascist government terminated the society for its decision and in the process provided Vieira with significant public recognition. The three stories that comprise *Luuanda* are among ten stories that were written between 1962 and 1964 in the jails of Luanda. Four other stories written at that time were published in 1974 by Plátano under the title *Velhas Estorias*.

Luuanda represents a transition in the development of Luandino Vieira. No longer content to write narratives in a linear time sequence, and unwilling to be bound by the confines of a standard Portuguese, Vieira creates a new direction in Angolan literature—a literature that will now reflect fully the language and spirit of the Angolan people. In fact, some of the dialogue in the stories of *Luuanda* is not an actual depiction of language as it is spoken in the musseques of Luanda, but rather a creation of Vieira that combines elements of spoken Portuguese with Kimbundu. In effect, he is enriching Portuguese by bringing to it an African originality that serves to assert the cultural independence of his native land. Angolan words such as "xingar" (to abuse, scold, revile) and "capim" (a tall yellow grasslike plant growing outside Luanda) are frequently used. And Vieira chooses to capture the particular resonance or lack of it of an individual speaker. "Milia" is used instead of "Emilia" and "tá rir" for "está rir"—phonetic reproduction matters more than correct spelling or grammar. But my knowledge of Angolan dialects does not permit me to deal in much detail with the revolutionary assault on traditional Portuguese by Luandino Vieira. It is sufficient to recognize that he is one of the founders of a "literatura angolana de expressão angolana."

Plot matters relatively little in the first two stories of poor people who struggle. In the first two stories, "Vavó Xixi e seu Neto Zeca Santos" (Vavo Xixi and Her Grandson Zeca Santos) and "Estória do Ladrão e do Papagaio" (Story of the Thief and the Parrot), most of the action takes place in the minds of individual characters. Through these characters, whose fears and sadness and dreams we share, Vieira presents a human comedy of life in the musseques. Zeca Santos, a boy who dreams of sleeping with and marrying Delfina comes to recognize that he is too poor and that he will lose her to João Rosa who has a good job and a car. Because Zeca's father is in jail as a terrorist, he can only get a backbreaking job at a cement factory that will hopefully provide him and his old grandmother with sufficient food to survive. Such a life leaves little room for girls or fancy clothes. The three thieves of "Estória do Ladrão e do Papagaio," a motley band of brigands, also know sorrow. The mulatto lad, o Garrido, who is lame, loves Inácia, his bosomy companion who is a servant for a white woman. O Garrido, weak and timid, is a virgin. In his dreams he enters worlds of delight that are unknown to him in his daily existence. But Inácia, who at times listens gently to his confessions of loneliness, teases him. She has many lovers, but with o Garrido she merely plays. The final torture occurs when she permits her pet parrot to hunt grapes between her breasts in the presence of o Garrido. In his search for food the parrot, Jaco, descends into her dress until it finds a reward between her thighs. Driven beyond endurance, o Garrido steals the bird that has always teased him about his limp, but before he can kill it, he is found out.

João Miguel, the leader of the group, lives in fear of any close human contact. Even excessive use of diamba (marijuana) cannot help him forget the day he was at the railway depot when his friend Felix was killed in an accident. Feeling that he was at fault, João Miguel seeks to flee from himself but is unable to erase the past. Only once he forgets; he comes to like o Garrido, but his guilt is too great—he must insult and curse o Garrido in order to stymie his feelings of warmth. In the process, poor o Garrido overhears himself called a "half-man" by his dearest friend, João Miguel, and the two friends face each other full of self-loathing.

Dosreis, a black Cape Verdean, an older man, fails in his attempt to steal seven ducks. Why steal ducks? There is no other employment for him in the musseque. He can give the ducks to the white man, Kabulu, who can sell them on the black market. Since Kabulu's brother has connections with the police, he never spends time in jail while Dorsais and o Garrido are frequent visitors to the cell.

In the third tale, "Estória da Galinha e do Ovo" (Story of the Hen and the Egg), two neighbors squabble about the ownership of an egg. Nga Zefa claims the egg is hers because the hen Cabíri that laid it is hers. Corpulent Bina claims the egg is hers because not only did she feed the hen, but the egg was laid on her property. A vigorous debate ensues in which all of the women of the neighborhood participate. After Dona Bebeca, the old lady, fails to resolve the conflict, various wise men are brought in to present their opinions on the subject. Sô Zé says that the egg actually should belong to him, for he provided the grain that fed it and has not yet been paid for it by Bina; Azulinho, the young religious scholar, advises that what is Caesar's should be rendered unto Caesar and what is God's should be rendered unto God, but that the egg belongs to neither Caesar nor God; o Vitalinho from whom Bina rents her home, claims the egg is his since the egg was laid on his property; o velho Lemos, a former legal assistant, regularly kicked out of his home by his wife, Rosália, so she can earn some money as a prostitute, offers a solution—a trial. But his plan is rejected once he charges various legal fees to all concerned so that he can buy a drink or two. In the end, Bina keeps the egg; Nga Zefa keeps her hen and the police who break up the public gathering are foiled in their attempt to keep the hen for themselves.

"Estória da Galinha e do Ovo" is a modern parable in which Vieira employs qualities of traditional oral storytelling. The theme of the trickster, the use of symbolism and proverbs, and a surprise resolution of the conflict can be found in the oral literature of many African societies. The Igbo writer Obioma Eligwe, in *Beside the Fire*, has also succeeded in recreating traditional tales in such a way that they have relevance to the contemporary political and social realities both in his native Nigeria and in other African countries.

"Estória da Galinha e do Ovo" must be seen as a satire of society in Luanda and throughout Angola. Bebeca, Sô Zé, Azulinho, o Vitalinho and o velho Lemos represent, respectively, traditional wisdom, the merchant class, the "enlightened" church, the landowner and the legal profession. Each fails in his attempt to contribute to the solution of the dilemma of the egg (the future of Angola). The arrival of the police (an obvious symbol of Portuguese military presence needed to preserve colonial interests) precipitates a sudden climax. The egg is no longer the sole issue; the ownership of the hen (Angola) herself is at stake. Throughout the story, two boys, Xico and Beto, have been playing with the hen, while the elders' debate continued. When they see that their friend Cabíri is in the hands of the police sergeant, Beto remarks:

É isso Xicô! Esses gajos não vão levar a Cabíri assim à toa! Temos de lhes atacar com a nossa técnica![6]

And this Xico! These guys are not going to carry Cabíri out just like that! We've got to attack them with our own technique!

Beto imitates the crow of a rooster, a trick he learned from Sô Petelu; a frenetic Cabíri flies from the grip of her alien captor and harmony is restored. Vieira is saying that it is the youth of Angola who must determine the future of their country, for the older generation has failed to recognize that without flexibility and innovation traditional wisdom cannot deal effectively with modern problems. Moreover, personal selfishness and dishonesty will help neither the individual nor the society as it seeks to live in a new age with new and different problems. There can be neither stability nor progress unless the people and their leaders are united in their desire to create a just society for an independent Angola.

In *Luuanda*, Vieira shows us the anonymous people of the musseques whose lives are not the subject of newspaper or magazine articles. He portrays their basic dignity, their individual value and in so doing, he creates a world that is completely human. The lives of these poor people matter; their small joys and small defeats matter. It is an African world where the community decides issues of importance; where fathers and husbands are in jail for opposing a colonialist regime and where the spoken language is not that heard in Coimbra or Lisbon. Underlying the stories is the theme of poverty that results primarily from job discrimination. As such, each of the stories in *Luuanda* is a work of protest and like the earlier works of Luandino Vieira reflect the author's committed stand.

During a one week period in April of 1967, while a prisoner at Tarrafal Concentration Camp in Cape Verde, Vieira wrote his second novel, *Nós, os do Makulusu*. Vieira himself has described his fifth work as a closed, circular narrative in which the author-narrator weaves in his memory the life of a family of colonists in a district of Luanda, persons who live the great problems—love and death—in the meshes of racism, colonialism, poverty, war—open wounds in the land of Angola.

The novel is an extended prose poem, a symphony of the mind in which certain phrases and themes reappear to be developed again. *Nós, os do Makulusu* is a sustained evocation of the music, smells, flowers, birds, paths, cafes, meals, rain, sun, and mist of years spent in Luanda, particularly of a childhood spent in the musseque of Makulusu. It is also a philosophical meditation on life and death and truths and falsehoods. The white narrator, called Mais-Velho (Older One) by Maninho, his beloved mulatto half-brother, comes to reject the comforts and arrogance of bourgeois life as a dangerous lie. He sees the sterility of a bourgeois twentieth century, an age of plastic and pills, where even death has no meaning. In fact, on several occasions, echoing Pablo Neruda in his monumental poem "Las Alturas de Macchu Picchu," Mais-Velho imagines an archaeologist of the future examining bones of twentieth century man and finding such a man to be an emasculated, blind, sad and stupid creature who was much less dignified, much less interesting, than those men of the Andes who lived thousands of years ago a primitive but more humanly generous existence.

Nós, os do Makulusu is above all a sadly joyful celebration of "nesta nossa terra de Luanda," a phrase that repeatedly punctuates the novel with its sad resonance. In this political novel, the narrator, at age fourteen, comes to recognize that the culture of the black and colored peoples of Angola is not at all inferior to that of Portugal. He learns that class struggle is at the root of social injustices and he comes to believe that "condições económicas de vida iguais, o preconceito racial desaparece como fumo!" (Economic conditions of life being equal, racial prejudice disappears like smoke). He learns that intelligence and commitment alone can redress the evils in Angola that have grown during five centuries of colonialism. He sees colonialism as a lie that stifles what is best and decent in oppressor and oppressed alike.

The death of dear Maninho, a second lieutenant, slain in an ambush by an anonymous shot, is a source of great grief to Mais-Velho. It is an especially inappropriate death, for Maninho did not even have the chance to die in combat. For his mulatto younger brother, war meant equality—in war, all are equal. Death is not a white man or a black man. The very nature of the liberation struggle was a manifestation of human equality in Angola.

There is a sad portrait of Mais-Velho's mother. She, who is poor and has worked hard all her life, cannot understand the nature of colonial exploitation; her life is simple—work and love of family. In rejecting his Portuguese society, the narrator knows feelings of guilt, for in hurting his mother, he hurts a good woman whom he loves. She has suffered. Her husband, Paulo, fathered an illegitimate son, Maninho. She loved that son who died in his youth.

Paulo, a colonialist who came from Portugal in the early 1950's, is a racist. He slanders black people at random. On his deathbed he is infuriated when Maninho's African mother is brought into the room; he orders "essa puta" (that whore), "essa negra" (that black woman), out of the room. This ignorant man, so sure in his ignorance, resents the fact that his children spend his money on books. He particularly resents the church school because the teacher is a black man. Paulo curses his own relative poverty that forces him to send his children to such a school.

There are many other interesting characters in *Nós, os do Makulusu*: Rute, the mulatto companion of Maninho who knows love because she knows death; Kibiaka, the dignified black militant who knows the songs of different birds; Maninho, himself, who fought out of love of Angola rather than any hatred of whites—what he hated was the destruction of love caused by colonialism; Maria who wore nylon stockings and made love in such a passionless manner that sex with her was death rather than life; Brito, the white metal worker who brutally kills a black child when an angry mob cannot control its venom. Locked in the cemetery of his discontent, o Velho, the thinker, the scholar, sees the sad plight of his land, for even though he is white, he is one of "os do Makulusu." In his dedication to the struggle, in his love for the land and its people, he is a brother to Maninho and all the people of Angola. *Nós, os do Makulusu* is another affirmative novel of love, of a very sorrowful love.

In his second novel, his most autobiographical work, Luandino Vieira abandons completely the concept of linear time that existed in different degrees in his earlier works. He has carried out a technique that he first used successfully in "Estória do Ladrão e do Papagaio." The resonance of his language, the felicitous combination of an aphoristic and a descriptive prose, mark this novel as a successful stage in the artistic life of Luandino Vieira.

* * * *

In Luandino's most recent book of three short stories, *No Antigamente na Vida* (Towards a Former Life), published in 1974 by Edições 70, political statements and social commentary are absent; rather we are taken into a different world, the magical and fanciful realm of childhood that can only be recaptured through memory. In this carefree universe a boy can journey by kite to the promised land, Tetembuatibia (the Kimbundu word for evening star), or he can fall in love with a fairy child with the otherworldly name of Urania. Whether or not his peers believe him does not matter, for a child knows a truth of imagination that cannot be destroyed by incredulous lads whose perceptions are already bound by the adult world of practical observation.

The theme of childhood has long fascinated Luandino. His first published book, a collection of ten stories, *A Cidade e a Infancia*, (The City and Childhood), is written in a direct, unadorned prose. These simple recollections of childhood experiences and observations are the work of a young author in his late teens and early twenties. When, in *No Antigamente na Vida*, Vieira returns to a subject that attracted him as early as 1954, he abandons altogether his simple narrative, for his vision of the world of childhood has grown more complex as Luandino has grown as an artist. Both collections of short stories are profoundly autobiographical. Luandino himself in a letter to me commenting on *No Antigamente na Vida* states that: ". . . eu sofria realmente e sentia realmente todas as emoções e aqueles factos como se se estivessem a passar no momento em que os verdadeiros (tão prosaicos!) se passavam!" (. . . I actually suffered and actually felt all those emotions and circumstances; as if I were reliving the very moments (so prosaic!) in which they took place.)

In *No Antigamente na Vida* Luandino conveys the unrestrained freedom of childhood through a language that is not limited by conventional usage. He invents words as if Portuguese had the word building capacity of German. "Brancaflor" is a white flower, for how can one separate the color "branca" from the "flor?" The rays of the sun are "se divididindo," breaking up in different directions—the standard "se dividindo" will not do, for extra syllables must be added to show the many rays of the sun. Stretching sands cannot be adequately pictured through "areias" which merely means "sands," for it does not give us a word picture of the sands that go as far as the eye can see. Vieira instead chooses "areias, reias, eias." By cutting off one letter after another, we can better see the receding perspective from the eye of the viewer. The reflection of eyes looking at one another is conveyed in "E eu olhei os olhos nos olhos dos olhos meus dentro dos dela." The image is so clear that the sentence does not need translating. In these stories Vieira has gone beyond his previous attempts at forging a language unconstrained by standard Portuguese expression. Throughout *No Antigamente na Vida* Kimbundu and Crioulo words abound; but it is in his use of neologisms and willingness to see language as a dynamic means of perception that makes these stories a significant contribution to modern literature.

Footnotes

1. Letter from Luandino Vieira to author, August, 1975.

2. Tomás Jacinto, "The Art of Luandino Vieira," *Ba Shira,* Vol. 5, no. 1, Fall, 1973, pp. 49-58.

3. In Castro Soromenho's novel, *Terra Morta,* the white colonialist administrator, Joaquim Américo resigns in protest against the policies and conduct of the Portuguese in Angola. Like Silvester, Américo's sympathies are with the oppressed and the exploited.

4. The Portuguese political police known for its brutal methods of repression which caused it to be compared to Hitler's Gestapo.

5. Luandino Vieira, *Vidas Novas,* (Vila da Maia, Afrontamento, 1975), pp. 89-90.

6. José Luandino Vieira, *Luuanda* (Lisbon, Edições 70, 1972), p. 185.

AGOSTINHO NETO AND THE POETRY OF COMBAT

Agostinho Neto is one of the few Lusophone African writers with an international reputation. He has spent much of his life in the struggle of his people to win independence. Whereas some Angolan intellectuals chose to live in Europe during the thirteen years of guerrilla warfare, Neto remained in his homeland organizing resistance to Portuguese domination. Moreover, Neto did not isolate himself from the great masses of Angolans living outside urban centers. He personally visited interior sections, eating with the people and frequently sleeping in their mosquito infested huts. For Agostinho Neto his own life has taken on meaning only in conjunction with the lives of the oppressed peoples of Angola.

Born in September, 1922, in the village of Kaxikane in the region of Icolo e Bengo about forty miles from Luanda, Neto was raised in a Christian household. His father was a Protestant pastor who like Neto's mother was also a teacher. After finishing his high school work in Luanda and working for a while in the Health Service, Neto went to Portugal in 1947 to study medicine at the University of Coimbra. He later transferred to the University of Lisbon. Like other African intellectuals, Neto quickly became involved in political activities. He was first arrested in 1951 and sentenced to three months imprisonment in Caxias, several miles west of Lisbon, for gathering signatures for the International World Peace Conference in Stockholm. He would return to Caxias in 1955, sentenced this time for two years. Neto's reputation as a poet brought particular attention to his case. Jean-Paul Sartre, André Mauriac, Nicolas Guillén and Diego Rivera were among those voices protesting his incarceration. Somehow, in between prison and writing poetry, Neto managed to complete his medical training and received his degree in 1958.

With his wife Neto returned to Angola where he was given a position of leadership within the M.P.L.A. When Portuguese authorities arrested him again in June 1960, and transferred him first to Cape Verde and later to Lisbon, protests were voiced from men and women who feared for his life. C. Day Lewis, Basil Davidson, Doris Lessing, John Osborne, Angus Wilson, Iris Murdock and Allan Sillitoe published a letter of protest in *The Times*. Penguin Books edited a book entitled *Persecution* by Peter Benenson in which Neto's case was examined. Moreover, International Amnesty became involved in the plight of Agostinho Neto. Bowing to such strong international opinion, Portuguese authorities released him in 1962 upon condition that he remain in Portugal. In July, 1962, Neto escaped and returned to Africa where in December of that year he was elected president of the M.P.L.A., a position he has held to the present time.

Neto's importance in Lusophone Africa has been compared to that of Léopold Senghor in Francophone Africa. Such a comparison is not without merit. Both Neto and Senghor are political figures who used poetry as a weapon in the struggle of African peoples to assert the originality, dignity and beauty of African cultures. Both négritude poets abandoned their literary careers, however, once they became political leaders. Neto and Senghor share a vision of a world of peace, love, brotherhood and harmony. Each man has received attention throughout Africa and much of the rest of the world. But there are marked differences as well between the two. Neto's prison experience and his activity in the resistance movement find no parallel in Senghor's life. Nor is the theme of political independence present in Senghor's négritude poetry whereas it constitutes a principal motif in Neto's poems of the late 1950's and 1960. Finally, the lushness of Senghor's imagery, the resonance of his line, is in contrast to the simpler, less descriptive language of Neto that ultimately moves us more by the message than by the rhythm of the poetry itself. It would be worthwhile for a detailed comparative study to be made on the poetry of these two men, but such an examination lies outside the scope of this book.

In 1961 Casa dos Estudantes do Império in the Colecção Autores Ultramarinos published a small volume of Neto's poetry under the title *Poemas*. A much larger selection appeared first in Italy in 1963 under the title *Con Occhi Asciutti (With Dry Eyes)*. This book was later published in Yugoslavia, Russia and China. The first complete Portuguese edition came out in 1974 as *Sagrada Esperança*, (Sacred Hope), the title Neto preferred. It was awarded the Poetry of Combat Prize by the University of Ibadan in 1975. The forty-eight poems in this collection constitute nearly all of Neto's poetic work and cover a period from 1945 through 1960.[1]

The theme of night is dominant in Neto's early poems; it is not the vi-

Agostinho Neto

brant exuberant African night that Senghor celebrates, but a somber time of ignorance, fear and death.

It is night when Manuel leaves his wife to be taken to São Tomé to do forced labor in "Partida para o contrato" (Departure for Forced Labor):

> Não há luz
> não há estrelas no céu escuro
> Tudo na terra é sombra
>
> Não há luz
> não há norte na alma da mulher
>
> Negrura
> Só negrura... [2]

> There is no light
> There are no stars in the dark sky
> Everything on earth is darkness
>
> There is no light
> There is no north star in the soul of the woman
>
> Blackness
> Only Blackness

The departing boat merges with dark sea and the dark sky which reflect the darkness in the soul of Manuel's wife.

At night in the musseque of Sambezanga, a district of black men and women, death comes in the form of a white policeman who beats a man mercilessly. The people seek an explanation for such murders and the taking of prisoners; the only answer is that they are black.

The poet is a prisoner of darkness. In the poem "Noite" (Night) he laments the misery of his condition:

> Eu vivo
> nos bairros escuros do mundo
> sem luz nem vida.
>
> São bairros de escravos
> mundos de miséria
> bairros escuros.
>
> Onde as vontades se diluíram
> e os homens se confundiram
> com as coisas.[3]

I live
in the dark quarters of the world
without light, without life.

They are slave quarters
worlds of misery
dark quarters
Where desires have been diluted
and men have been confused
with things.

The people of the musseques struggle to survive. The shopkeeper in "Quitandeira" (Shopkeeper), sitting under a mulemba tree outside her stall to avoid the direct rays of the hot sun, cries out to a passing lady that the oranges she has for sale are good. But she has not spent her life merely selling fruit—she has given up as well her spirit that has been trampeled by her hard life.

Compra laranjas doces
compra-me também o amargo
desta tortura
de vida sem vida.

Compra-me a infância de espirito
este botão de rosa
que não abriu

E ái vão as minhas esperanças
como foi o sangue dos meus filhos

Aí vão as laranjas
como eu me ofereci ào alcool
para me anestesiar
e me entreguei as religiões
para me insensibilizar
e me atordoei para vivir.[4]

Buy sweet oranges
Buy from me also the bitterness
of this torture
of this lifeless life.

Buy from me the innocent spirit
this rose bud
that did not open

And there go my hopes
like the blood of my own children

There go my oranges
just as I delivered myself to drink
to anesthetize myself
in order to become insensitive
and I made myself dizzy in order to live.

A rose bud that never opened, a life of fruitless sacrifice—the quitandeira need not feel alone. Another quitandeira in "Meia-noite na quitanda" (Midnight in the Shop) works beyond midnight to earn money so her son can pay taxes. Gathering her individual tostões (a tostão is worth ten centavos or approximately a quarter of a cent), Sá Domingas must earn ten thousand reis or one hundred escudos, about four dollars. So she sits outside calling out:

Cem réis de jindungo
Cinquenta réis de tomate
Três tostões de castanha de caju[5]

One hundred reis for pepper
Fifty reis for tomatoes
Three tostões for cashew nuts

Neto presents a gallery of victims in his early poems. Forced labor, hunger, loss of dignity, loss of hope, humiliation, even death, assault the body and spirit of the African living under colonialist domination. Life in the musseques is "ansiedade" (anguish). There is "saudade (nostalgia) dos dias não vividos" (of days never lived) in "Sábado nos musseques" (Saturday in the Musseques). But Neto does not despair. In the very first poem of *Sagrada Esperança*, "Adeus a hora da largada" (Farewell at the Hour of Departure), he asserts his faith in himself and the people to create a new destiny. Blind hope offers no hope; change can only be effected through individual and collective action:

Sou eu minha Mãe
a esperança somos nós[6]

I am my Mother
Hope—it is us

This is the sacred hope of an Angolan future in which justice and human dignity will replace bondage and excoriating humiliation. Neto identifies with the people. In "Sombros" (Shadows) shadows pass before him of manacled convicts who were dragged away to die; all the suffering of Africans who lived under imperialist domination in the past becomes shared in the present. There is no "I"; there is only "we." Past and present are merely paths leading to a certain future.

Neto recalls his childhood friend Mussunda in three of his poems, but it is in "Mussunda Amigo" (Mussunda Friend) that he best captures the quality of that friendship which is symbolic of the bond uniting all oppressed Angolans.

> Contigo
> Com a firme vitória da tua alegria
> e da tua consciência
>
> > O ió kalunga va mu bangele!
> > O ió kalunga va mu bangele-lé-lelé...
>
> Lembras te?
>
> E escrevo versos que não entendes
> compreehendes a minha angústia?
>
> Mas no espirito e na inteligencia
> nós somos!
>
> Nós somos
> Mussunda amigo
> Nós somos [7]

> With you
> with the firm victory of your happiness
> and your conscience
>
> > O ió kalunga va mu bangele!
> > O ió kalunga va mu bangele-lé-lelé...
>
> Do you remember?
>
> And I write verses you don't understand
> Do you understand my anguish?
>
> But in spirit and comprehension
> We are one!
>
> We are one
> Mussunda my friend
> We are one

Although Mussunda did not go to school and therefore cannot read the poems of Agostinho Neto, in his spirit and in his thinking, he too shares the vision of a better day. The Kimbundu phrase was spoken by Mussunda who recognized in his friend a potential leader or guide of the Angolan people. The first of the two lines is best translated "And you were created by destiny." The second line echoes the first but suggests that Neto's ideas of liberty and justice, which he voiced as a boy in conversation with Mussunda, are rooted in a distant past, the "lé-lelé" at the end of this line indicates a past more remote than the simple past tense of the first line. "Kalunga" has several meanings in Kimbundu—sea, death, or destiny; each one possesses the quality of being endless. "Kalunga" is frequently negative, but in "Mussunda Amigo" it is an affirmative destiny, ineluctable as death or the sea, a destiny of freedom and peace.

That "Kalunga" can also be destructive and cruel is apparent in Neto's short story "Nausea," which was first published in *Mensagem* in 1952 and later included in Fernando Mourão's anthology *Contistas Angolanos*. In this sad tale, velho João, the youngest son of a fisherman, who rejected his father's profession in order to gain more money hauling sacks for the white man in Luanda, comes to regret the choice he made. While visiting his sick brother on an island near Luanda, velho João escapes the stifling heat of his cubata in Samba Kimôngua where he lives in the suburbs. The clean air, the soft sand and the smell of the ocean bring him a sense of peace that he has not had in a long time. After a good lunch, he strolls along the shore with his young nephew.

The sea is kalunga, the sea is death. The endless sea with monstrous sharks that devour man has brought misery to many fishermen. The sea took his grandfather to another continent; the sea took the life of his cousin Xico who died when his canoe overturned and he drowned. But if the sea is kalunga, so also is it life for the African in Luanda:

> O trabalho escravo é kalunga . . . kalunga é a fatalidade . . .
> Trouxe o automovel o jornal a estrada. . . . A civilicação ficou embora ao pé da praia, a viver com kalunga. E kalunga não conhece os homens. Não sabe que o povo sofre. So sabé fazer sofrer.[8]

> Slavish work is kalunga . . . kalunga is fate. It brought the automobile, the newspaper and roads . . . Civilization remained at the foot of the beach to live with kalunga. And kalunga doesn't know men. It doesn't know that people suffer. It only causes suffering.

The lures of urban life created by the Portuguese are like the lures of the sea. Beneath an attractive surface there is only inevitable suffering.

The happy mood of velho João vanishes. He feels nauseous. Looking away from the sea at the tidy asphalt road leading to the city, he vomits his lunch. His nephew helps him return to the house and thinks that his uncle has, like other old men he knows, drunk too much. The nephew does not understand the significance of "O mar. Mu'alunga!" When velho João spoke these words aloud, the boy silently listened, waiting for an explanation and when it did not come, he paid no attention to the utterings of the old man. How could he have known what life was like before Luanda had grown into a metropolis? How could he have known the disappointment that kalunga brought to velho João?

The fate of velho João cannot be changed, but the future of his nephew will not be so degrading. A new day is dawning. It is expressed in the tormenting rhythm of the tom-tom that beats out a clear message:

> Ninguém nós fará calar
> Ninguém nos poderá impedir
>
> Vamos com toda a Humanidade
> conquistar o nosso mundo e a nossa Paz.[9]

> No one will silence us
> No one can impede us
>
> We are going with all humanity
> to conquer our world and our peace.

These lines from "A reconquista" (The Reconquest) announce a renunciation of an African past that has been ravaged and raped by facades of democracy and Christian equality; they announce a victory over poverty that causes prostitution, over the intimidating weapons of the white colonialist, over a past in which everything traditionally African was denigrated.

A new day is suggested through images of flowers and fruit, springtime and birth. The rosebud that remained unopened in "Quitandeira" blossoms in "Mãos esculturais" (Sculptured Hands) and in "Um bouquet de rosas para ti" (A Bouquet of Roses for You). The roses are sweetness and freshness, happiness and friendship, strength and sureness, but most of all, life:

> Um bouquet de rosas para ti
> —rosas vermelhas brancas
> amarelas azuis—
> rosas para o teu dia
> e Vida! para o teu dia[10]

A bouquet of roses for you
—roses of red, white
yellow blue—
roses for your day
and Life! for your day

After a pan-African conference in Bamako, Mali, in 1954, Neto writes:

Bamako!
ali nasce a vida

Bamako!
fruto vivo da África
de futuro germinando nas artérias vivas de África

Ali a esperança se tournou arvore
e rio e fera e terra
ali a esperança se vitoria amizade
na elegância da palmeira e na pele negra dos homens[11]

Bamako!
there life is born

Bamako!
future fruit of Africa
of a future germinating in the live arteries of Africa

There hope was transformed into a tree
and river and heart and land
there hope applauds friendship
in the elegance of the palm tree and in the black skin of men

 A new Angola, an Africa reborn cannot find inspiration in Europe; it must above all look to Africa's past, to Africa's traditions, to Africa's values to create a vigorous African future. Western civilization did not bring enlightenment but only slavery and misery. In "O verde das palmeiras da minha mocidade" (The Green of the Palm Trees of My Youth) Neto recalls his own childhood; the Cuanza river flows through his mind; he thinks of marvelous prophecies of the sorcerers and of objects transformed into gods. Images of mysterious secret sects and oral stories recounted around a fire dance before him. And then he remembers how he left this Africa to discover a world his friend Mussunda would never know, the world of Europe, of Beethoven. The alienated Neto seeks to return to the world he left when he came to Luanda. This feeling is best expressed in the stirring poem "Havemos de voltar" (We Must Return):

Às cases, às nossas lavras
às praias, aos nossos campos
havemos de voltar
Às nossas terras
vermelhas do café
brancas do algodão
verdes dos milharais
havemos de voltar
Às nossas minas de diamantes
ouro, cobre, de petróleo
havemos de voltar
Aos nossos rios, nossos lagos
às montanhas, às florestas
havemos de voltar
À frescura da mulemba
às nossas tradições
aos ritmos e às fogueiras
havemos de voltar
À marimba e ao quissange
ao nosso carnaval
havemos de voltar
à bela pátria angolana
nossa terra, nossa mãe
havemos de voltar

Havemos de voltar
À Angola libertada
Angola independente[12]

To the homes, to our tillage
to the beaches, to our fields
we must return

To our lands
red with coffee
white with cotton
green with maize fields
we must return

To our wealth of diamonds
gold, copper, petroleum
we must return

To our rivers, our lakes,
to our mountains, to our forests
we must return

To the coolness of the mulemba
to our traditions
to the rhythms and to the fires
we must return

To the marimba and to the quissange
to our carnival
we must return

To the beautiful Angolan homeland
our land, our mother
we must return

We must return
to Angola liberated
to Angola independent

This poem was written in Aljube prison in October of 1960. At that time many African countries colonized by the British and French were achieving independence. But the Portuguese were unwilling to give up their hold on Lusophone Africa. Neto can no longer be satisfied to speak merely of love and harmony and brotherhood; no longer can he think in terms of an undefined future. Dignity demands full political independence as quickly as possible. The hoisting of an Angolan flag, victory in the struggle that has gone on for five centuries, must be achieved.

The poems written in 1960 are poems of combat. The poet speaks of the impending battle. A sense of impatience and agitation is present. In "Depressa" (Immediately) Neto rejects one biblical posture—the turning of the other cheek—in favor of another—an eye for an eye, a tooth for a tooth!

e vindimem folhagens e frutos,
para derramar a seiva e os sucos sobre a terra húmida
e esborrache o inimigo sobre a terra pura
para que a maldade das suas vísceras
fique para sempre aí plantada
como monumentos eternos dos monstros
a serem escarnecidos e emaldicoados por gerações
pelo povo martirizado durante cinco séculos.[13]

and gather grapes, leaves and fruit
to scatter the sap and juices over the moist earth

and squash the enemy over the pure earth
so that his inner evil
may remain forever fixed there
like eternal monuments of monsters
to be scorned and cursed for generations
by the people made martyrs for five centuries.

Angolan heroes of earlier ages who fought the Portuguese are praised for their courage which is shared by those descendants who will not fear death, for individual death is but a path to new freedom for Angola. Ngola Kiluanji and Rainha Ginga, Kimbundu Legendary figures, stand side by side with the people who may be named Benge, Joaquim, Gaspar, Ilídio or Manuel. Wave upon wave will stand up against the enemy, for the land and the people together cry out—"Independência!"

"A Voz Iqual" (Equal Voice), the last poem in *Sagrada Esperança*, synthesizes the themes of Neto's poetry. The black man who built Western empires in Africa, the laborers who were sacrificed so Europe could plunder Africa's coffee, diamonds, oil—these men were given nothing in return except ingratitude and cruelty. Africa, which gave its rhythms to America and its bodies to the international athletic community, rejects a past in which Europe was glorified and Africa was debased. With independence a future of dignity and pride is to be created, nourished by the roots in the ancestral humus of Africa. A return to Africa's past is the best way to purify the continent of alien cultures and to reconstruct a modern African society. There will be a collective sharing of joys and sorrows, for workers will work side by side in the fields for the benefit of the entire community. Africa will take her place as an equal in the modern world. She will contribute her energies to create a harmonious world in which brotherhood among men becomes a reality.

The battle will be hard, but there will be no tears. With determination and a new found confidence the Angolan people will create their destiny. Like his first poem, Neto's final poem is a departure. From 1961 to 1976 he has been a military and political leader guiding the M.P.L.A. in the long and difficult battle for independence. The military successes of the guerrilla fighters in Angola as well as in Mozambique finally were rewarded. The Portuguese military, tired of a war they could not win and unwilling to continue fighting so a few wealthy people within Portugal could profit, revolted and on 25 April, 1974, the revolution suddenly overthrew the fascist Caetano government in Lisbon. On October 1, 1974, General Costa Gomes, the President of the Republic, declared that he would personally direct negotiations leading to the decolonization and independence of Angola. On November 11, 1975, Angola became an independent nation. And once again, there is another beginning for Angola.

The language of Neto's poetry is nearly always simple and direct. It is seldom colloquial, in contrast to the popular poetry of Jacinto. Occasional Kimbundu words and expressions do serve to create an African ambiance not merely in subject matter but in spirit as well. A call for courage in Kimbundu

> Xi ietu manu
> kolokota
> kizuua a ndo tu bomba
> kolokotenu[14]

> Our land
> courage
> a day will come in which
> the enemy will have
> to ask pardon of us

is a particularly African appeal. But Neto does not write in Kimbundu for several reasons. He himself is much more competent in Portuguese and those Angolans who can read are much more likely to know Portuguese than Kimbundu.

In his imagery, sparse as it is, Neto brings to his poems the people, landscape, trees and animals of different parts of Angola. Life in the musseques is recreated as well as life in the countryside. Those in the kinaxixi (public market place in Luanda), the women of Lunda, the Bailundos (an Umbundu people of the South around Sá da Bandeira), and the Kiocos (a vibrant people in the Northeast section of Angola famous for its diamonds) are brothers in the struggle. The umbundeiro trees, the valleys, the giboía (a cobra), the virgin forests of Maiombe—this is the Angola that Neto loves. Nevertheless, the poet cannot completely suppress that part of him that has been westernized. When Neto writes of the glorious struggle of the people which produces music in his soul, he entitles the poem "Sinfonia." An unconscious betrayal perhaps, but certainly African music could have provided a more appropriate title. He goes to Europe for an image in "Assim clamava esgotado" (Thus They Cry Out Exhausted) comparing African innocence drowned in slavery to Shakespeare's Ophelia, a victim not only of her innocence but her own betrayal of Hamlet. Such imagery does not seem appropriate, for few of Neto's Angolan readers would even know the sad story of Polonius' daughter.

The short lines of the early poems are replaced by much longer lines in some of the later poems, for in these Neto uses many more adjectives and adjectival phrases. Nevertheless, in nearly all his poems the rhythm is created by repetition of word or phrase. Like a drum beating out a message, the repetitious pattern of the sounds of the words gives the poem an internal unity of form. In "Havemos de voltar", the series of prepositional phrases beginning each stanza with "to the", accompanied by the beat of "havemos de voltar" at the end of the stanzas, creates a sense of urgency and discipline.

At times Neto can be lyrical, especially when he speaks of his beloved:

> Sonharei
> sonharei com os olhos do amor
> encarnados nas tuas maravilhosas mãos
> de suavidad e ternura.
> Sonharei com aqueles dias de que falavas
> quando te referias à Primavera:
> Sonharei contigo
> e com a prazer de beber gotas de orvalho
> na relva
> deitado au teu lado,
> ao sol-uma praia furiosa lá ao longe.[15]

> I will dream
> I will dream of your loving eyes
> incarnated in your marvelous hands
> of sweetness and gentleness.
> I will dream of those days in which you spoke
> when you thought of Springtime;
> I will dream of you
> and of the pleasure of drinking dewdrops
> in the grass
> lying at your side,
> in the sun—a savage coast there in the distance.

But Agostinho Neto does not often write of an individual love—that is a luxury; he writes about his love of his people, of his land and of liberty. And he writes primarily for his people. Unlike the Francophone Négritude poets whose voices were heard more in Europe than in Africa, men like Neto, Costa Andrade, and António Jacinto brought their words to their own market place where the Angolan people came to know them. Many of Neto's poems have been put to music by soldiers who would sing these hymns of Africa. Poems such as "Havemos de Voltar" and "Criar" (Create) are particularly well known. Ruy Mingas, among others, put out a record of Neto's poems and his songs can be heard in the streets of Luanda today, for in Neto's words the dreams of Angola are expressed.

Footnotes

1. I know of one Neto poem, "Fogo e Ritmo" (Fire and Rhythm), that is not contained in *Sagrada Esperança;* probably there are others.
2. Agostinho Neto, *Sagrada Esperança* (Lisbon, Livraria Sá da Costa Editora, 1974), p. 37.
3. *Ibid.*, p. 56.
4. *Ibid.*, pp. 49-50.
5. *Ibid.*, p. 53.
6. *Ibid.*, p. 35.
7. *Ibid.*, pp. 79-80.
8. Agostinho Neto, "Nausea" in Fernando Mourão, *Contistas Angolanos* (Lisbon, Casa dos Estudantes do Império, 1960), pp. 57-58.
9. *Sagrada Esperança*, p. 85.
10. *Ibid.*, p. 110.
11. *Ibid.*, pp. 92-93.
12. *Ibid.*, pp. 127-128.
13. *Ibid.*, p. 124.
14. *Ibid.*, p. 114.
15. *Ibid.*, p. 99.

GERALDO BESSA VICTOR
AND THE VOICE OF A GENTLE NEGRITUDE

Geraldo Bessa Victor, a lawyer by profession and a poet by inclination, was born on January 10, 1917, in Luanda. His father, a Catholic who converted to Protestantism after his marriage, worked for a company which supplied iron parts for trains and truck engines. One of five children, Bessa Victor completed his secondary schooling in Luanda. From 1937 to 1946 he worked for the Bank of Angola, after which he left Luanda for Portugal where he enrolled at the Facultade de Direito of the University of Lisbon, graduating in 1951.

Bessa Victor is the author of six volumes of poetry—*Ecos Dispersos* (Scattered Echoes) 1941, *(Ao Som das Marimbas* (To the Accompaniment of Marimbas) 1943, *Debaixo do Céu* (Beneath the Sky) 1949, *Cubata Abandonada* (Deserted Hut) 1958, *Mucanda* (Message—in Kimbundu) 1964, and *Monandengue* (Child—in Kimbundu) 1973. He has also written a book of short stories *Sanzala sem Batuque* (Home without Music) 1967, and various essays on Angolan culture. His most recent studies, *Ensaio Crítico Sobre a Primeira Colecção de Provérbios Angolenses* (Critical Essay on the First Collection of Angolan Proverbs), and *Intelectuais Angolenses dos Séculos XIX and XX—Vol I—Augusto Bastos* (Angolan Intellectuals of the 19th and 20th Centuries) were both published in 1975. Gaston-Henry Aufrère, in a volume entitled *Poèmes Africaines* has translated twenty-nine Bessa Victor poems into French; my own English translations of selected poems have appeared in the literary journals *Okike* and *Ba Shiru*.

The négritude poetry of Bessa Victor is rooted in the poet's identification with his African past and the dream of a future in which brotherhood will replace bigotry and love will transcend hatred. The mucanda or message of these poems is not primarily political—Bessa

Victor has successfully eschewed the temptation to write a poetry of propaganda without abandoning in the least his intimate attachment to the culture, language and spirit of Africa. As an African poet of négritude, he does not shout; he does not cry out—rather he sings sad songs of human folly and canticles of joy. A profound melancholy is nearly always present in these lyrical verses, but it is a melancholy that ultimately is vanquished by a wonderful elan expressing the hope of a new day in which man will cease to be dominated by his lower instincts. Like the African people, who after mourning the death of their beloved chief break into celebration in order to overcome their grief, Bessa Victor's poetry serves to assert the need for personal and collective optimism at a time in history filled with sadness and tragedy.

Children and childhood constitute a central theme in the poetry of Bessa Victor. In *Mucanda*, which is divided into three parts, the initial section of eight poems is entitled "Menino Negro" (Black Child). All of the poems in *Monandengue*, written nearly two decades later, are concerned directly or indirectly with experiences of childhood. These songs of innocence celebrate the spontaneity and natural warmth of children whose pure world frequently has yet to be polluted by the egoism and sophistication of the world of adults. Black children and white children can play together without any consciousness of a difference in color as in the poem "Apontamento na Quitanda do Muceque" (Note on a Shop in the Muceque):

    Na quitanda do muceque
    de S. Paulo de Luanda
    o menino negro chupa sorvete
    o menino branco come quitaba,
    ambos sorrindo, ambos cantando
    a *Maria Candimba*, o *Abril em Portugal.*

    E a minha alma de poeta
    —alma mestiça, luso-tropical—
    descobre acenos de África
    no gesto do menino branco
    e visões da Europa
    no olhar do menino negro.[1]

    In the shop in the muceque
    of S. Paulo de Luanda
    a black child is sucking sherbert
    a white child is eating quitaba,
    both smiling, both singing
    Maria Candimba, April in Portugal.

Geraldo Bessa Victor

And my poet's soul
—a hybrid soul, luso-tropical—
discerns signs of Africa
in the gesture of the white child
and visions of Europe
in the look of the black child.

The black child and the white child are not aware of racial or cultural differences. Europe and Africa coexist—there is no superior or inferior culture, but rather a happy fusion of two cultures. Bessa Victor believes that the Portuguese, more than the French and English, created a symbiosis of European and African values. Not only was the black man integrated into Portuguese culture without completely losing his intrinsic African being, but an environment was created in which the white man, through his contact with life in the interior of Africa, could identify with African values and sentiments. What else could explain the fact that a white poet from Ribatejo, Vieira da Cruz, in *Quissange*, *Tatuagem* and *Cazumbi*, sang of the black Angolan, of his customs and traditions.[2] In fact, in the summer of 1975 when I was in Lisbon seeking out African literature written in Portuguese, I was advised by an African friend, a former guerrilla leader of the M.P.L.A., that I should purchase the poetry of Vieira da Cruz for, I was told, he is among the greatest of Angola's poets.

Bessa Victor's vision of a cultural harmony is neither a romantic dream nor a rejection of his African past. He realizes that although the vast majority of people are blinded by their narrow perspective and self-interest and consequently are unable to embrace the thoughts or values of another society, this is not true for all men. The historical commingling of Portugal and Africa has resulted in a unique situation that has produced not only a Vieira da Cruz but a Rui Knopfli, an António Jacinto and a Castro Soromenho, among other white writers who have chosen to identify with Africa without totally neglecting their European heritage.

The children of "Apontamento na Quitanda do Muceque," growing up in the outskirts of Luanda, sharing food and music, smiling and singing together, are fortunate, for they have yet to come to look at the world in terms of black and white. This is not the case with the children in "O Menino Negro Não Entrou na Roda" (The Black Boy Did Not Enter the Circle). In this poem a black child comes across a group of white children playing in a circle, singing festive songs. A white boy, spying the black child invites him to join in:

'Venha cá, pretinho, venha cá brincar'
—disse um dos meninos com seu ar feliz.

a mamã, zelosa, logo fez reparo;
o menino branco já não quis, não quis . . . .³

'Come here, black friend, come play'
said one of the children with his happy air.
His mother, solicitous, made a comment;
the white child no longer wanted, no longer wanted . . . .

The intrusion of the adult world destroys the child's natural fraternal instinct. But the poet refuses to identify with the racial posture of the white woman. He realizes that her knowledge is the product of unfortunate societal influences. In "Crianças" (Children) Bessa Victor asserts his conviction that love can destroy those barriers separating blacks from whites, that love can create a fraternal bond uniting all people:

Nem meninos negros nem meninos brancos
mas meninos.
Nem cânticos de escravo nem canções de senhor,
mas apenas hinos
de amor.

Nem palavras de ódio nem ameaças loucas
(não, nunca ameaças!),
mas apenas braços que geram abraços,
mas sòmente bocas
que fecundam beijos onde o corpo e a alma
não conhecem cores, não conhecem raças.

Nem criancas brancas nem crianças negras!
só crianças,
que não tem raça, que não tem cor,
Nelas se fundiram todas as alianças
do amor!⁴

Neither black children nor white children,
but children
Neither canticles of the slave nor songs of the master
but only hymns
of love.

Neither words of hate nor crazy threats
(no, never threats!)
but only arms that beget embracing,
nothing but mouths

that make fruitful kisses where body and spirit
are ignorant of color, and race.
Neither white children nor black children!
only children,
without race, without color.
In them are cast all alliances
of love!

In the poems about children Bessa Victor sees love and the knowledge of love as the total victory of freedom over slavery, of the goodness and glory of life over grief, despair and folly. Bessa Victor is also the poet of love between man and woman. In *Cubata Abandonada* and *Mucanda* the sounds and perfumes of Africa are made manifest in the seductive and bewitching body of the African woman. The voluptuous anticipation of love-making in "Esperando a Noite" (Waiting for Night) and the awakening of love in "Na Noite de Batuque" (In the Night of the Batuque) are rooted in the Africanness of the lovers. Bessa Victor can be a poet of sensuality, but his eroticism is never exaggerated or vulgar and consequently is never offensive. There is frequently a lyrical agitation in this poetry. As always in Bessa Victor, there is sadness. Around the fire where the batuque is danced the poet's body and spirit are warmed by his lover; his sorrow is assuaged:

O ritmo da vibrante orquestração
de marimbas, cacochas e tambores,
vem transformar em prazer
a dor das nossas dores.

Nestas transmutações por que passamos,
na noite de batuque, em gozo e dor
somos seres fadados pelos deuses
para criar e fecundar o amor.[5]

The rhythm of the vibrant orchestration
of marimbas, cacochas and drums,
is transforming into pleasure
the depth of our grief.

In these transmutations through which we pass,
in the night of the batuque, in joy and grief
we are beings destined by the gods
to create and produce love.

Sexual love is a means of transcending grief and celebrating life. Ultimately the poet realizes that pure spontaneous love between man and woman, like the spontaneous love of children, is a triumphant expression of what is best in man. In "Amor sobre a marca da negritude" (Love on the Seal of Negritude) the African poet, addressing his African lover, warns that their love must go beyond their Africanness:

> Mas não invoques só motivos rácicos
> para este amor tão espontâneo.
> Sobre a marca da negritude
> há o selo do humano.
>
> Assim, ó minha amada,
> vem para os meus beijos, vem para os meus abraços,
> vem para a comunhão dum amor
> maior que o amor da raça![6]

> But don't invoke only racial causes
> for this love so spontaneous.
> On the seal of negritude
> there is the stamp of the human.
>
> Thus, my love,
> come receive my kisses, come receive my embraces,
> come receive a communion of a love
> greater than the love of race!

The ritual of love in these poems is a ritual of life in which the black man and woman experience a profound communion with all men and women who love in cities and villages, in palaces and huts, in Africa and throughout the world.

Bessa Victor's affections are not directed solely towards children and lovers. In "A Velha Mulemba" (The Old Mulemba) he remembers the old Mulemba tree under which as a boy he used to play and rest from the heat of the sun. When the tree was cut down he cried, for it was as if something vital and essential in him had been killed. The poet addresses the reader who accuses him of being sentimental. No one can understand his grief; the mulemba was his friend:

> —Uma vez, em criança,
> puxei os bigodes do meu avô velho;
> deu-me uma bofetada,
> que minha cara negra ficou logo encarnada.
> Pois, por muitos anos, eu andei puxando,
> dia a dia, as barbas da velha mulemba,
> nelas fiz balouço, fiquei balouçando;
> e a velha mulemba não ficou zangada,
> nunca me fez nada,

nem um só açoite, nem um só lamento,
senão a carícia das suas longas barbas
no meu rosto, no meu corpo, quando o vento
as beijava e fazia estremecer...

Minha velha mulemba...
Ah, so eu sei que me faz sofrer![7]

—Once, as a boy,
I tugged at the mustaches of my old grandfather;
he gave a slap,
so that my black face turned red.
So, for many years, day after day,
I used to pull the branches of the old mulemba,
Out of them I made a swing to play;
and the old mulemba never became angry,
never did anything to me,
not a single slap, not a single lament,
other than the strokings of the long beard
on my face, on my body, when the wind
was kissing and shaking it...

My old mulemba...
Ah! I alone know what makes me suffer!

The poet is on a higher level than the children or the lovers, for it is his consciousness and art that can give form to his vision. He has maintained his affirmative spirit and his sense of fraternity in spite of his knowledge of the world and his awareness that his message of brotherhood in all likelihood will be ignored. He sees himself as a vagabond spreading a life-giving love over deserts of human tragedy. With an open heart men and women of all colors and races are asked to overcome their enmity. The white poet and the black poet in "Poema da Fraternidade Frustrada" (Poem of Frustrated Brotherhood) sing songs of love and life, but the overwhelming silence of the masses of white and black people crushes the dream of the idealistic poets liberated from the suffocating bog of prejudice. But the poet must write to overcome grief in a world where even the purest of motives is suspect. In the poem "O Negro Vagabundo" (The Vagabond Negro) Bessa Victor refuses to be intimidated by those who do not accept him because their hearts are too sullied to understand him:

Eu vou nesta viagem pelo mundo.
E há vozes que perguntam: — Quem é ele?
Há uma voz que responde: —É um vagabundo;
uma força secreta, estrahna, o impele.

Vou por caminhos de variados rumos.
E há vozes que perguntam: — Donde vem ele? Donde: . . .
—Vem de terras e mares ignorados,
há uma voz que responde.

Então canto os meus versos de poeta.
E mil vozes perguntam: —Que pretendes?
Que bens compras ou vendes?
Qual é a tua meta?

Donde vem o teu sonho e para onde vai,
nesta longa viagem?

Eis a Voz do Universo: —Em silencio, escutai,
mercenários da alma, calai vossa linguagem
de ganância e vaidade.
O poeta negro traz ao mundo uma mensagem
de amor e fraternidade.[8]

I go on this journey through the world.
and voices ask: —Who is he?
A voice responds: —He is a vagabond;
a secret and strange force impels him.

My journey takes me on various paths.
And voices ask: —Where does he come from?
A voice responds:
He comes from lands and waters unknown.

Thus, a poet, I sing my verses.
And a thousand voices ask: —What do you want?
What goods are you buying or selling?
What is your goal?

What is the source of your dreams? Where does it take you
on this long journey?

Here is the Voice of the Universe:
—Listen, quietly,
mercenaries of the soul, silence your voices
of cupidity and vanity.
The black poet brings to the world a message
of love and fraternity.

With the publication of *Monandengue,* Bessa Victor announced the end of his poetic career in order to devote more time to research and essays on Angolan culture and literature. But the poetic spirit cannot be silenced even by the fiat of the poet himself. He calls his most recent poem,

"Na Hora da Independência de Angola" (The Hour of Independence of Angola), a "postscriptum" to his poetic work. This poem was written in August, 1974, and appeared in the newspaper *A Provincia de Angola"* in Luanda several months later. Bessa Victor sees Angolan Independence as:

... a Hora em que, decerto, pela primeira vez,
o Branco há-de-tomar a iniciativa
de saudação fraterna,
numa nova manhã, sob o ceu angolense:
—'Bom dia, Negro!'—
E este 'Bom dia' há de sair do coração,
não dos lábios.
E o vocábulo 'Negro' ficará redimido
enternamente,
de toda a lama com que o mancharam,
de toda a injuria com que o violentaram,
durante tantos séculos.

...the hour in which assuredly, for the first time,
the white man must take the initiative
in a fraternal greeting,
in a new dawn, under an Angolan sky:
—'Good day, Black man!'—
and this 'Good day,' must come from the heart,
not just from the lips.
And the word 'Negro' will be cleansed
eternally,
from all the mud with which they stained it,
from all the injury with which they ravaged it,
for so many centuries.

The new dawn in Angola will be a time when the riches of the earth will be freed from the grasp of capitalistic monopolies so that the people can share in the natural wealth of their land. Men who were formerly enemies will embrace one another in a gesture of friendship. The vagabond poet continues to bring to the world a message of love and brotherhood.

An assessment of Bessa Victor as a poet is in order and to do so one must appreciate the nature of poetry itself. The quality of a poem is to a large extent independent of the subject of the poem. The meaning of the poem is not merely the subject but also the arrangement of sounds, rhymes, punctuation, structure, vocabulary and syntax. For this reason a good poem cannot be reduced to a simple prose rendering without destroying the life of the original. Since *what* a poem says cannot be separated from *how* the poem says what it says, one cannot simply praise Bessa Victor's humanism as superior art merely because his point of view transcends racial hatred and social bigotry. Certainly, the fact that unlike many African poets, Bessa Victor is not writing poetry to elicit a particular response from the reader or listener is to his credit. Any art which aims in advance solely to provide a single reaction must inevitably be rejected as inferior. Pornography, soap operas, television detective programs and propagandistic art are one dimensional; they do not appeal to an aesthetic or spiritual nature. Bessa Victor himself has defined authentic art as the "revelação de estado de alma das realidades vividas, das vivências experimentadas e sentidas" (revelation of the essence of realities that are experienced or felt).[9] Bessa Victor's poetry reflects his concern with experiences that are not limited to a single historical period or a single political perspective.

As an African poet writing in Portuguese, Bessa Victor has been praised by such critics as Alvaro Salema and Alvaro Dória as a modern master of the Portuguese language, as a uniquely original poet who, in expressing the nature and quality of his Africanness in a European language, has dominated that language to the point that he has few equals either in Africa or in Portugal.[10] His is no sterile Parnassian imitation of European forms, for Bessa Victor, in subject and sentiment, in sensibility and sensuality, is always an African poet. The lyrical gentleness of his négritude is manifested in the softness of the sounds of his words, in the simplicity of his language and in the extraordinary precision of his art. He is not complex and obscure like Wole Soyinka or Christopher Okigbo nor is his simplicity only the cry of social protest of an Ovídio Martins or some of the Francophone négritude poets. Like Senghor and Gabriel Okara at their best, Bessa Victor at his best is a genuine poet whose depth and resonance have transformed into a coherent art an originality and beauty nourished and rooted in Africa.

A very brief glimpse at "Apontamento na Quitanda de Muceque" illustrates Bessa Victor's art. The effective use of rhyme serves to unite the poet, the black child and the white child. The marriage of Europe and Africa is suggested by the rhyming of "Portugal" with "tropical" and appropriately the only final words ending in "o" in the second stanza are the words for white and black, "branco" and "negro." The Kimbundu word "muceque" rhyming with the European product "sorvete" further suggests the harmony that the poet perceives in the gestures and looks of the two children.

The very simple lines: "ambos sorrindo, ambos cantando a *Maria Candimba,* o *Abril em Portugal"* reinforce the dominant theme as well. These lines are perfectly balanced. The first line presents the image of two boys standing next to one another. The word "ambos" itself stresses the fact that the children are sharing an experience; the present participle conveys the immediacy of the scene. The African and European songs, each of seven syllables, one feminine and one masculine, accent the mood of order, peace and integration.

Perhaps Bessa Victor's vision is quixotic; perhaps his withdrawal from the political arena is to be condemned by some. But the poet voices a vision of human love, a vision that is needed today as desperately as at any time in the history of man. Perhaps in a distant future the warm words of this Angolan poet will no longer reflect a dream but an actuality. Bessa Victor's commitment is to human values; he appeals to the noblest sentiments of man. His songs, rooted in the traditions of an African humanism, disciplined with a craft he acquired in Africa and Europe, offer a glimpse of a better day. Like the South African writer Peter Abrahams, Geraldo Bessa Victor sees in personal love and friendship an emblem of a world that could be if man would listen with the heart and the mind, and triumph over his pettiness, stupidity and the arrogance of his ignorance.

* * * *

Bessa Victor's collection of short stories, *Sanzala sem Batuque,* was published by Editora Pax in Braga, Portugal, in 1967. It is difficult to render an exact translation of the title. "Sanzala" refers to a slum or district in which poor blacks live together in relative poverty. "Sem" is a preposition meaning "without"; "Batuque" is a native dance. It is a strange title, for none of the eight individual stories is called "Sanzala sem Batuque". What is implied by the title, however, is the loss of joy of a pure African culture in the suburbs of Luanda, the capital city of Angola, where most of the stories are set. It is a theme that recurs in many of the stories. The title, therefore, refers to this remembrance of things past, of a life that once was but is no longer. Bessa Victor generally concentrates on the lives of individuals who for one reason or another are unable to find fulfillment. Inertia, stultification and impotence trap his characters in a world where the future offers no hope of happiness or joy. More often than not, these suffering characters are aware of their sad plight. Bessa Victor nearly always sympathizes with his characters, even those who are not admirable. There is no acerbic rancor in his tone. We feel the same sense of compassion that we experience in reading some of his best poems, dramatic portraits of people and places that have known better or more glorious times.

A variety of themes appear in Bessa Victor's stories. Race prejudice is one subject that manifests itself in a number of ways. In the story "E Proibido Brincar" (Playing is Forbidden) the black child, Betucho, is one day rejected by his best friend, Carlitos, whose father, through the imprecations of a prospective son-in-law, determines that black children do not constitute desirable friends. To add to Betucho's disappointment, he later learns that Carlitos' mother had originally encouraged friendship between her white son and his black playmate. A more subtle but no less powerful expression of racial prejudice is found in such stories as "A Filha de Ngana Chica" (The Daughter of Ngana Chica) and "Duelo de Gigantes" (Giants' Duel) where black Africans seek self-respect only through denigration of those whose skins are darker. The psychological implications of such an attitude are staggering. Franz Fanon's insightful and provocative study, *Black Skin, White Masks,* explains this masochistic phenomenon in the minds of those blacks who feel that manhood or success can be achieved only through a process of "blanch-ification." Rejection of self and acceptance of white standards result in ultimate deception. Ngana Chica's world knows no values beyond the assumed superiority of whiteness over blackness. Her every action stems from monetary greed and a desire to be more "white" than her neighbor. Unfortunately, Ngana Chica's primary vehicle in impressing her friends is her lovely daughter, Regina, whose happiness is shattered by the machinations of her mother. Ngana Chica cleverly succeeds in destroying her daughter's relationship with her black lover, Raul, in order for her to be the mistress of the white engineer, Castro, who has left his family in Portugal while on assignment in Luanda. This is a sad story of a love that fails because of the selfishness and cupidity of adults. In these tales of racial prejudice among blacks, it is the mulatto who is the symbol of ultimate triumph:

> Um mulato é sempre olhado indubitàvelmente como pessoa civilizada, quer pelos brancos quer pelos proprios negros; mas um preto, ainda que muito educado e muito instruido, tem de prover primiero que é efectivamente civilizado, senão olham-no e tratam-no como um indígena qualquer.[11]

> A mulatto is always looked at indubitably as a civilized person either by whites or by black people themselves; but a black man, be he well educated or knowledgeable, must first prove that he is genuinely civilized, in order not to be treated as a nobody.

Another theme that recurs in the stories is that of cultural schizophrenia brought about through interaction with the urbanized white world. In "Domingas ou as Duas Faces da Alma" (Domingas or the Two Faces of the Soul), Bessa Victor narrates the plight of Domingas whose European education brings her a high standard of living, but at the same time she remains as isolated from the white world she has entered as she is from the African bush she has left behind. In this story there is a lengthy discussion on the sociological justification of the practice of "dowry" and "bride price" in the traditional Western and African societies.

A third theme, which occurs in many poems as well as several stories, involves illicit sexuality, usually between a white man and an African woman. Bessa Victor is obviously interested in the implications of such behavior. In 1970 Editora Pax published his essay *Quinjango no Folclore Angolense* (Quinjango in Angolan Folklore), a most fascinating study of an oral narrative which has evolved into a written ballad. There are several interpretations of the ballad, one by Oscar Ribas, another by Assis Junior. The subject of the story is a celebrated white military figure who fathers an illegitimate child with his black servant-girl. Bessa Victor points out that the offspring of such a union must be seen in its historical-sociological context, for thousands of mulattoes have become an integral part of Angolan society. In the story "A Filha de Ngana Chica" the daughter of Ngana Chica gives birth to a child fathered by the engineer, Castro. We are told:

> E, nos recessos de sua alma bruzuleante, soava de forma estranha, como funebres vozes de outro mundo, o eco vago de berro animalesco, brutalmente aleluítico 'É mula-to . . . É mula-to . . .'[12]

> And, in the recesses of her burning soul, sounded in a strange form like mournful music from another world, the vague echo of an animal lowing, brutally with hallelujah, 'he is mulatto . . . he is mulatto . . .

The oxymoronic "brutalmente aleluítico" expresses the ambivalence of her feelings—the joy of giving birth to a light skinned child and the horror of learning for sure that Castro, and not her lover Raul, is the actual father of the child.

The authenticity of indigenous African culture is a fourth theme in Bessa Victor's stories. Through the frequent use of Kimbundu words, metaphors and similies in which the imagery is often taken from African life — ". . . o comboio . . . iniciou a marcha no seu vibrante batuque de 'tuque-tuque'" (The train began its climb in the vibrant batuque 'tuque tuque')—through allusions, witchcraft, spiritism, and ancestors, and references to specific customs including bride price payments as well as festival dances and songs, Bessa Victor brings us into the Kimbundu world. He recognizes the integrity of a culture which, if different from Portuguese culture, is authentic and valuable in its own right.

Certainly the above mentioned themes are not unique to Lusophone African literature. On the contrary, African writers in English and/or

French from South Africa to Senegal, have written of racism, cultural schizophrenia, illicit sexuality and the essential value of autochthonous African culture. However, Bessa Victor appears to be particularly interested in the effects on society of the illegitimate children, fathered by light skinned men. Such a theme would not obviously be prevalent in the literature of people whose population included a mere handful of mulattoes.

There is one particular quality to Bessa Victor's work that directly or indirectly results from his exposure to Portuguese society. Many of his poems and some of the stories are tales of "saudade." Portugal is the land of "saudade," of a sad and gentle yearning after that which seems unattainable. Often it alludes to a nostalgic homesickness as well. The "fado" is the most obvious example of "saudade" in Portugal. It is worth noting that Roger Bastide directly suggests a relationship between Bessa Victor's "Langueur du fado portugais" and "le rhythme sonore du tam-tam africain". In *Sanzala sem Batuque* the word "saudade" appears in three of the stories, "O Comboio e o Navio" (The Train and the Boat), "Domingas ou as Duas Faces de Alma" and "Carnaval". In each case there is a slightly different quality to the "saudade."

"O Comboio e o Navio" is one of the two most successful stories in the collection. A majority of Bessa Victor's stories suffer from flatness of character. Only in this story and "Carnaval" is he able to avoid the temptation to subordinate completely individuality of character in order to reveal a certain theme or group of themes. "O Comboio e o Navio" is a story of "saudade."

Zito, an ambitious boy, determines to leave his native village of Cabiri where he has worked as a laborer for his brother-in-law for several years. Long hours of toil have been rewarded by a paltry salary. With minimal savings Zito boards the train that will take him to Luanda and to a new life of hope and opportunity. His fondest dreams are realized in the capital city; Zito acquires work in the home of a well-to-do family. He runs errands, takes their little girl to and from school, and works in the garden. He is well liked by the household, particularly by Victoria, the goddaughter, who enjoys flirting with him. Zito's world has undergone a distinct change. His earnings have increased eight fold; he sleeps on a bed instead of on the floor; his food is tasty. Luanda has proven to be a mecca for the African boy who deserted his native village to seek a better life in a modern city. After four or five years as a servant in Luanda, Zito is suddenly faced with a crisis. Dona Fernanda, his employer, is to leave for Lisbon and is willing to take Zito with the family on condition that he marry Victoria, who is in love with him. Poor Zito doesn't really love her, and although he has dreamed for years of going to Lisbon, he sadly refuses to join the family on their journey by boat to the Portuguese capital

Throughout the story Bessa Victor carefully depicts the emotional responses of Zito and other characters, for "O Comboio e o Navio" is, above all, an agonizing song of frustration and deep sadness. As Zito waits for the train that will take him from his home and family, he thinks "Saudades da terra natal? A saudade não ao Busca, ela è que nos cativa."[13] (Homesickness? Homesickness is not looked for, it is what imprisons us.); Zito finds that "saudade" is an enemy to be overcome. His mother bellows a cry of distress as the train pulls out of the station, carrying off her beloved son; the chug of the train echoes the profound grief in her heart. Similarly, when the boat taking Dona Fernanda's family to Lisbon departs, Zito senses a sadness much like that felt by his own mother on the day of his departure to Luana:

> O monstro marinho expeliu outro bramido, mais forte, mais fundo, mais longo. Momentos depois, começava a deslizar na imensa estrada de água.
> De olhos turvos, Zito olhava o oceano e o barco—e por ilusão só via o rio Bengo e o comboio, e só ouvia alucínadamente o angustioso grito materno: —Aiué, Zito![14]

> The sea monster ejected another howl, stronger, deeper, longer. Moments later, it began to slip into the immense avenue of the sea.
> With turbid eyes, Zito gazed at the ocean and the ship and through an illusion, he saw only the river Bengo where he often played as a boy and the train, and all he heard in his hallucination was the agonizing maternal cry:
> —Aiué, Zito!

Zito himself has become trapped by the "saudade" that he tried to escape. In the end he has replaced his mother as the isolated figure who watches the departure of something cherished and desired. The sense of despondency is conveyed through the final sentences. "Mais forte, mais fundo, mais longo" with the repetition of the "mais" and the long vowel sounds suggest the depth and degree of Zito's suffering. The "o" (pronounced "oo" in Portuguese) sounds in the last paragraph not only suggest the bellowing of the ship's horn but also the lowing of Zito's spirit. The "o" cry is often a dominant sound in Portuguese "fado," for it carries within it a message of sadness, of "saudade."

The theme of "saudade" in "Domingas ou as Duas Faces da Alma" is presented in a much less subtle manner than it is in "O Comboio e o Navio". Domingas, an Angolan girl, is raised by the white Silva family who serve as her god-parents. They provide her with every opportunity to enjoy the fruits of the good life. She goes to Portugal with them and eventually becomes a successful and relatively well-to-do secondary school teacher. However, as time passes she finds herself without a husband. Frustrated and dejected, Domingas finally agrees to marry a man old enough to be her father, who not only is very poor but has twice been arrested for minor misdemeanors. To make things worse, Domingas does not love him.

Domingas' fate is contrasted with that of her uneducated sister, Maricota, still living in the African bush. Maricota has married a wealthy man who gave her a considerable bride price of two thousand angolares, six pieces of cloth, three sacks of flour, twenty litres of wine, and an ox. Bessa Victor suggests that for all her education, Domingas has not fared as well as Maricota. Domingas longs for her lost past:

> Sentia saudades da mãe e da irmã, e do
> Anastácio, como nunca experimentara:
> sofria com saudade de terra natal.[15]

> She felt a longing for her mother and
> sister, and Anastácio [a white man who in
> the past wanted her as his mistress] as she
> had never before experienced: she suffered
> a homesickness for the land of her birth.

Unfortunately, Domingas' plight fails to win the sympathy of the reader. In the first place, she is under no obligation at age twenty-six to marry anyone. Secondly, there is no reason to assume that an intelligent black woman in Western society is condemned to be rejected by men of a similar level of intelligence and social standing. Thirdly, her choice of husband reflects her own lack of self-respect. Fourthly, we are led to believe that Domingas spent years of studying to become a teacher merely to gain social standing. There is no reference to her concern for students or to her gaining any pleasure from intellectual experience.

"Domingas ou as Duas Faces da Alma" is a contrived story that fails to achieve its desired purpose. Bessa Victor sets out to show the plight of the modern European educated African who can neither fully reject his African past nor completely accept the values of Western civilization. This is a familiar theme in African literature that has been developed successfully by many writers including Cheikh Hamidou Kane (Senegal), Camara Laye (French Guinea), Wole Soyinka (Nigeria), Kofi Awoonor (Ghana), Ousmane Sembène (Senegal), and Chinua Achebe (Nigeria).

Bessa Victor's story fails not because his message is incorrect, but rather because Domingas, as the principal character, is not adequately developed.

The eighth and last story in *Sanzala sem Batuque*, "Carnaval," is a tale of "saudade." The narrator returns during festival week to his native Angola after a long absence in Portugal only to find that the Africa he once knew has all but disappeared. It is possible that the narrator in this story is Bessa Victor himself, as we are told he is a lawyer. The carnival itself is the central figure, for it symbolizes all that has happened in the interim. Where formerly there was bustling activity, traditional celebrations, and a singular ambiance, there exists only a paltry caricature of the past:

> Está tudo mudado. As ruas estão vazias, mortas, sem esses grupes folclóricos, tradicionais que, com as suas marchas, os seus trajes espaventosos, os seus pendões policrimos, os seus imperadores e 'imperadoras', os seus reis e reinhas, os seus hinos deliciosamenta toscas e ingénuos, os seus ritmos rebombantes, as suas pelejas de rivalidad sempre estimulada, povoavam e agitavam Luanda e subúrbios.[16]

> It is all changed. The streets are empty, dead, without these folkloric, traditional groups, that, with their marches, their terrifying costumes, their polychrome pennons, their emperors and empresses, their kings and queens, their deliciously coarse and ingenuous chants, their resounding rhythms, their contests of rivalries that are always stimulating, filled and excited Luanda and its environs.

Now passionless parades of automobiles have usurped the day. The narrator can only conlude that "Não há carnaval" (It is not carnival); he is filled with remorse for a way of life that can be recaptured only in his imagination:

> Recolho a mim mesmo, à minha memória, ao cofre recôndito da minha alma, em chamamento duma saudade viva que em sonhos responda a esta saudade morta.[17]

> I collect for myself in my own memory, in the recondite coffer of my soul, a summoning of a genuine 'saudade' that in dreams responds to this dead 'saudade'.

A tone of gentle sadness is felt throughout "Carnaval." One senses that the author feels a need to sing his own fado of his native land that has changed so much in a short time. I am reminded of Camara Laye's *Dramouss* in which the author recounts his own disillusionment at returning to his homeland after years of study and work in Paris. Like Laye's novel, Bessa Victor's story is a confession of love. And like the Guinean novelist, Bessa Victor creates memorable portraits of people and events of the past.

In "Carnaval" there are two such characters. One is Zita, the girl whom the narrator left behind and pledged to marry upon returning. Their first meeting, their vows, their emotions are recaptured in a simple lyrical recollection. Although the memory of Zita remains firmly entrenched in his mind, the fact remains that the narrator and she have gone separate ways. The "saudade" of Zita echoes the "saudade" of his Angola.

A second and wonderful character is Tio Domingos, "o Carpenteiro," the narrator's uncle who, because he was black, was always treated as an inferior by the narrator's mulatto family. Sentiments of remorse overwhelm the returning lawyer when by chance he meets his old uncle in the Bairro Operario. He recalls with guilt and sadness the racism in his own family. His uncle was never called "tio" but always "o Carpenteiro," the carpenter. Whenever guests came, "o Carpenteiro" was always forbidden to appear. The narrator learns that his uncle, a man who has known much humiliation, was in his youth a hero of one of the "Entrudos." In fact, an anonymous folk song sings the glory of the triumphant "Rei da Famosa" who vanquished "O Imperador da Caridade" in a contest involving the respective leaders and their gangs. But alas, this erstwhile king is but a poor lonely old man who has only memories of a single moment of triumph. Like the beggar in the poem, "Rei Destronado," (Dethroned King) Tio Domingos symbolizes a lost and admirable past that seems out of place in the modern world. Bessa Victor's odyssey has resulted in a profound "saudade" of another time and another way of life. "Carnaval" is a prose poem of "saudade," an African fado of a departed love, a departed glory, and above all, a departed spirit.

Footnotes

1. Geraldo Bessa Victor, *Monandengue* (Lisbon, Livraria Portugal, 1973), p. 37.

2. Geraldo Bessa Victor, "Problemática da Cultura Angolana," (Boletim da Sociedade de Geografia de Lisboa, Jan.-March-April-June, 1973), p. 57.

3. Geraldo Bessa Victor, *Mucanda,* second edition (Braga, Editora Pax, 1965), p. 14.

4. *Ibid,* pp. 25-26.

5. *Ibid,* pp. 41-42.

6. *Ibid,* p. 38.

7. Geraldo Bessa Victor, *Cubata Abandonada,* second edition (Braga, Editora Pax, 1966), p. 26.

8. *Mucanda,* pp. 73-74.

9. "Problemática da Cultura Angolana," p. 56.

10. Dória's essay "Um Poeta da Négritude" which appeared in *Gil Vincente,* Aug., 1966, expresses the view that Bessa Victor is a truly great poet, superior even to Senghor, and that his art will endure the trials of time.

11. Geraldo Bessa Victor, *Sanzala sem Batuque* (Braga, Editora Pax, 1967), pp.52-53.

12. *Sanzala sem Batuque*, p. 26.

13. *Ibid*, p. 66.

14. *Ibid,* p. 71.

15. *Ibid,* pp. 82-83.

16. *Ibid,* p. 107.

17. *Ibid,* p. 109.

MÁRIO ANTÓNIO AND THE FACE OF EUROPE

Mário António Fernandes de Oliveira, scholar, poet and writer of short stories, was born in Maquela do Zombo, Angola, on April 5, 1934. He completed his primary and secondary studies in Luanda. After spendng eleven years as a public civil servant in the Angolan capital, he came to Portugal in 1965 and has remained in Lisbon since that time. He is presently employed by the Gulbenkian Foundation.

An active participant in the literary journal *Mensagem*, Mário António began writing serious literature of quality in his middle teens. *Poesias*, his first collection of poems, came out in 1956; it was followed by *Amor* (Love), 1960; *Poemas e Canto Miúdo* (Poems and a Short Canto), 1960; *Chingufo—Poemas Angolanos,* 1962; *100 Poemas,* 1963; *Era, Tempo de Poesia* (Era, Time of Poetry), 1966; *Nossa Senhora da Vitória de Massangano* (Our Lady of Vitoria de Massangano), 1968; and *Rosto de Europa* (Face of Europe), 1968. Besides his three volumes of short stories and his poetic contributions to literary journals over the past two decades, Mário António, an indefatigable researcher, has contributed many essays on Angola and Lusophone African literature and culture in the nineteenth and twentieth centuries. He is one of Africa's outstanding intellectuals.

It is the paradox of Angolan literature that a white man, Luandino Vieira, has not only written novels and stories about black and mulatto people of the musseques, but has also been inspired by traditional African oral literature, while the poetic voice of Mário António, a mulatto, is frequently in harmony with a chorus of confused twentieth century European writers who have withdrawn into the abyss of the solitary self in order to explore multifarious layers of perception. Vieira's world is communal; Mário António's world is a private demesne in which abstract images suggest endless labyrinthine corridors.

This was not always the case. In his early years Mário António wrote in the language of the people of Luanda about the lives of the people with whom he identified. In his introduction to Carlos Eduardo's collection, *Poetas Angolanos*, (Angolan Poets) published in 1959, Mário António states that:

> A poesia tradicional dos povos de Angola é uma realidade riquíssima e viva... é uma poesia *socialmente enquadrada e servindo fins sociais*.[1] Ela está presente em quase todas as manifestações de sabedoria popular, quer associada ao canto, quer subjacente às diferentes formas de literatura oral: conto, provérbio, adivinhas.[2]

> Traditional poetry of the peoples of Angola is a very live and rich actuality... it is a socially framed poetry serving social ends. It is present in almost all manifestations of popular wisdom, whether associated with song or underlying the different forms of oral literature: fable, proverb, riddles.

In his essay he further asserts that Angolan poetry is not based on rational systems as is the poetry of Europe. African poetry does, however, follow certain rules of stress and meter, and parallelism in particular is a common device found in traditional proverbs, riddles and poems.

"Avó Negra" (Black Grandmother), written in 1950, is an African poem rooted in an African ambiance. Mário António, like the traditional poets of his homeland, uses poetry to serve social ends:

> Minha avó negra, de panos escuros
> da cor do carvão
> Minha avó negra, de panos escuros
> que nunca mais deixou.
>
> Andas de luto,
> Toda és tristeza
>
> Heroína de ideias,
> rompeste com a velha tradição
> dos cazumbis, dos quimbandas.
>
> Não chinguilas no óbito
> Tuas mãos de dedos encarquilhados
> tuas mãos calosas da enxada
> tuas mãos que me preparam
> mimos da nossa terra
> (quitabas e quifututilas),
> tuas mãos, ora tranquilas,
> desfiam as contas gastas
> de um rosário já velho.
>
> Já não sabes chinguilar
> não fazes mais que rezar.
> Teus olhos perderam o brilho.
> E da tua mocidade

Mário António

só te ficou a saudade
e um colar de missangas.

Avózinha, às vezes
ouço vozes
que te segredam saudades
da tua velha sanzala

de cubata onde nasceste
das algazarras dos óbitas
dos sonhos do alambamento
que supunhas merecer.

E penso que
se pudesses
talvez revivesses
as velhas tradicões!³

My black grandmother, in dark clothes
color of carbon
My black grandmother, in dark clothes
which she never gave up.

You go in mourning,
All is sadness:

Heroine of ideas,
you broke with the old tradition
of cazumbis and quimbandas.

You don't chinguilar in death,
your hands with wrinkled fingers
your hands, hardened from the hoe
your hands which prepared
gifts from our land
(quitabas and quifufutilas),
your hands, tranquil, now,
untwist the beads worn
for the rosary grown old.

You no longer chinguilar,
all you do is pray.
Your eyes have lost their glitter.
And from your youth
you only kept a nostalgia
and a necklace of missangas.

Dear grandmother, at times
I hear voices
that whisper to you memories
of your old sanzala

of the cubata where you were born
of the cries of the dead
of the deceitful temptings of the quimbanda
of the dreams of alambamento
that you thought to deserve.

And I think
if you could
perhaps revive
the old traditions!

The poet laments the grandmother's dependence on the Christian religion while she has neglected the traditional wisdom of her people. The Kimbundu words which seem so foreign to the non-African reader are symbolic of an essence that has become foreign to the old lady, who has exchanged a world of "cazumbi" (souls of the dead), quimbandas (witch doctors), missangas (beads) and alambamento (bride price) for rosary beads. The word "alambamento" itself suggests a certain degree of alienation from a pure African past. The original Kimbundu word for bride price, "Ku lemba," becomes "alembamento" and subsequently "alambamento."

In another early poem, "A História Triste" (Sad Story), written in 1951, the poet, looking into the eyes of a girl, is inundated by their sense of mystery:

E vi
E vi filas de escravos no sertão
E vi negros chorando no porão do negreiro.

E ouvi
E ouve ruído das correntes
E os gritos das mães sem filho
E das amadas sem noivo.

E os meus labios se abriram
temerosos
Para contar a grande história
A história triste.[4]

And I saw
And I saw rows of slaves in the bush
And I saw black men crying in the holds of slave ships.

And I heard
And I heard the sound of running
And the screams of mothers without sons
And sweethearts without fiancés.

And my lips were opened
Fearful

To tell the great history,
A sad history.

A sad history indeed. The repetition of the verb in the first two of these stanzas suggests the repeated injustices and suffering that the West brought Africa. The fact that eight successive lines begin with "e" reinforces the idea that these crimes carried out over centruies constitute a long history of sadness for African peoples. The poet, who saw in his mind's eye lines of slaves being led either to their early deaths or to a life of perpetual degradation, feels obliged to tell the story of Africa. Images of black corpses thrown into the sea from the slave ships, of shrouds of green, appear in another early poem, "A Procura de um Poema" (The Search for a Poem), of 1951.

This is Mário António, the African poet, immersed in the history and culture of his African past. But there were indications in the early 1950's that the voice of the poet would become more and more private. In "Chuva" (Rain), Mário António sings of an ideal love of the imagination that does not permit him to love a particular girl.

Essa chuva é minha amante
Velho fantasma meu:
Inutil, meu amor, tua presença.[5]

That rain is my beloved
My longtime phantom:
Useless, my love, your presence.

The sadness of Africa's history is less immediate here than the sadness of love lost, or hope destroyed. He remembers his dead father, his schoolmate killed by a speeding car in the Rua da Maiange, and the old African lady who can no longer comfort him. They are all gone and he is alone, accompanied only by dreams of love that by their very nature cannot be realized. In "Do Amor Impossivel" (Of Impossible Love), the poet, living in that country of tears and mist "dentro de cada um de nós" (within each of us), finds that the journey toward love fulfilled is never ending.

Da separação de nós
Que nunca fomos nós
Mas eu e tu:
Tu ela, tu alheia, tu distante.[6]

Out of the separation of us
Who never were us
But you and I:
You—she, alien and distant you.

The love poems of Mário António are, for the most part, very melancholy. The poet's own perceptions are necessary for a woman's loveliness to be captured, but all too often such loveliness must be measured against an ideal that can never be matched. There is, at times, a softness to the texture of certain lines that lingers after the poem is ended, such as in "Não Invoquei o Sonho para Amar-te" (I Didn't Invoke the Dream In Order to Love You) where the poet speaks of the relationship between his art and the woman he loves:

> Perfeito a harmonioso é o que dá-se
> Entre quem és e o esforço de cantar-te.[7]

> Perfect and harmonious is what results
> Between who you are and my effort to sing of you.

In some poems love is harmony, order, peace, but never for long. The poet's dream of oneness, of integrating his life into the world that surrounds him, is as impossible as his visions of idealized love.

He longs for order:

> —Um dia, do meu ser dividido
> Reclamareis a unidade
> Conclamando os espíritos sobre mim,
> Velhas mulheres negras do meu sangue![8]

> —One day, out of my divided self
> You will demand unity
> Calling together spirits upon me,
> Old black woman of my blood!

The divided self of Mário António does not find unity. The poet, alienated from a world created by his own imagination and alienated from the mundane world of everyday existence, goes to Europe, but his alienation is only increased because his self comes to know a further division—that between Africa and Europe.

In *Rosto de Europa* (The Face of Europe), Mário António's most recent book of poems, the poet rejects completely his earlier contention that African poetry is communal in nature. An impressionistic aesthetic, apparent in the later poetry of Mário António, is articulated by a character in one of his short stories who, in talking about painting, could be talking about poetry:

> Ele sabia que, aos olhos das pessoas de mente clara, aquele pedaço de praia não existia. . . Sabia quo o quo existia era

um continente e que, remetendo-se a um certo plano—aquele que os valores são realmente operantes—um continente não tem praias, nem paisagens, nem banhistas solitários; um continente se organiza como uma grande composição abstructa, onde manchas que se corporisam, traços que se alongam, acabam impondo ao artista um sentido, um movimento, uma reposta, que são os seus propios. E que, no quadro, cada ponto da composição só fica valendo em função disso, da sua integração no todo... Era apenas uma questão de símbolos.[9]

He knew that in the eyes of clear minded people, a particular part of the beach did not exist . . . He knew that what existed was a continent and that, placing himself on a higher plane—that in which values are truly operating—a continent does not have beaches nor landscapes, nor solitary bathers; a continent is organized like a great abstract composition, where spots that solidify, lines that stretch out, end up imposing on the artist a feeling, a movement, a response, that are his very own. And that, in the painting, each dot of the composition has value only in this, in its integration into the whole . . . It was only a question of symbols.

The poetry of Mário António has become more and more a verbal portrait of a place, a mood or an experience captured by a series of apparently gratuitous images which, when combined, present a feeling, a movement, a response. This is an aesthetic not too far removed from the dominant direction of much European poetry since the time of the Symbolists. *Rosto de Europa* is European in subject and in style. To be more exact, the poems in this volume generally reflect a portrait of Portugal rather than one of the European continent. Mário António describes Lisbon from the other side of the Tejo as a Nude Maya painted by the brushes of the sun, which captures its sensual body. Évora at dusk is captured in a series of images:

Céu violeta, firmes estrelas.

Exsuda cal o tronco
sobre a terra rossa.

Um vinho doce lava
o sarro de borrego
em nossa boca.

Évora ao longe. Olivos!
Paredes brancos de luar.[10]

Violet sky, fixed stars.
The trunk exudes lime
over the red earth.
A sweet wine washes down
the lamb skin
in our mouths.
Évora from a distance. Olive tree!
White walls in the moonlight!

There is no mention of the flowers in pots hanging from the windows of many of the homes of Évora. Nor is there an image of the most impressive legacy of Roman civilization in Portugal, the beautiful Temple of Diana standing near the cathedral. The selected images are combined in such a way that the taste of lamb and the color of the sky form part of a single composition, a unique picture of one of Portugal's more attractive cities.

Many of the poems in *Rosto de Europa* are abstract. In "Braille," the poet, closing his eyes, feeling the texture of the braille script, this "caligrafia de experiências longínquas" (caligraphy of distant experiences), goes on an imaginary journey to remote places where images of pine trees, the wind, and the clear water of a continent merge.

Mário António captures the spirit of the fado in "Fado":

Garganta, xaile, garganta
O corpo molda-se em voz
E a voz sem corpo no ar!

Candeeiros destacam rostos
Mais rostos: os que pedem
os que troçam, os que imploram
os que ameaçam. . .

Faces diferentes do amor!
De ancas largas, maternal,
De pequenos seios castos
Até o amor assexuado.

Da garganta às ancas
- Mil faces do amor
No movimento de um xaile
Canta-se o fado.[11]

Throat, shawl, throat
The body molds itself to the voice
And the bodiless voice to the air!

Lamps reveal faces
More faces: those that beseech
those that mask, those that implore
those that threaten. . .

Different faces of love!
Large hips, maternal,
Small chaste breasts
Including asexual love.

From the throat to the hips
- A thousand faces of love
In the movement of a shawl -
The fado is sung.

    The fado is not merely the music; the fado is also the ambiance of the people and the singer—the faces, expressions, and movements which combine to create a particular atmosphere. Body and voice, singer and listener, merge in this poem celebrating this sad music of Portugal. Anyone who has heard the fado sung in a Portuguese environment knows that the contact between those making the music and those listening to it is an essential ingredient; when a fado singer performs in front of a foreign audience, the essential Portuguese ethos of the experience is completely lost.

    That Mário António, an Angolan, chooses to be inspired by European models and subjects in his poetry, does not negate the quality of his art. But certainly the African poet of "Avó Negra" and the European poet of "Fado" are different poetic voices, nourished by different roots. It is not surprising, therefore, that the later poetry of Mário António is more or less neglected by Angolans while such work is praised in the West as a significant contribution to the development of the culture of his homeland. In fact, one noted critic points out that only through such a writer as Mário António, a poet concerned neither with race nor color, a writer universal in scope, does Angola make a lasting contribution to literature. Unfortunately "universal" is used here as a synonym for that which is valid for the West. Mário António, the poet, more praised outside Africa than within, does not contribute to Angolan culture by abandoning his identity with Angola. Europe has its own writers; African writers have sufficiently vigorous cultural traditions that they need not look elsewhere for their roots. To do so is to betray themselves and their society.[12]

* * * *

    Mário António, however, never completely left Africa. An examination of his short stories, particularly the three volumes published in the middle 1960's, indicates that at times he has felt a need to follow the advice given Avó Negra—to return to the old traditions. The truth in the early stories is social; the committed African writer rooted in his society is a spokesman for that society.

Poverty, loss of dignity, and the rhythm of day to day life are principal themes in the story "O Cozinhiero Vincente" (Vincente the Cook), written in 1952. Vincente confides in his son Néné the unhappiness of his life:

> E a sua conversa era a desculpa da sua condição de negro bebado, a acusação contra todos os que o censuravam sem o compreender. Contra a patroa que lhe não aumentava a salário com o pretexto de que o gestaria todo no vinho.[13]

And his conversation was an apology for his condition of a drunken black man, an accusation against all who criticized him without understanding him. Against his boss who did not give him a raise under the pretext that he would waste it all on wine.

Once he was imprisoned; they cut his hair and beat him. Néné recalls how he and his father would sit down and cry together. Poor Vincente, dominated by drink, suffers various physical setbacks until finally his continual spitting of blood necessitates his staying at home. Sá Domingas, his wife, a washerwoman in Luanda, does not make enough money to provide adequate medical care. She too cries and Néné sees that "através das lágrimas, os olhos da mãe eram os mais suaves e amorosos do mundo."[14] (through the tears, mother's eyes were the most sweet and loving in the world.) Even nature seems to weep, for the twilight is described as full of "sangue e lágrimas" (blood and tears).

Feeling that the death of her husband is near, Sá Domingas begins to scream hysterically, more to attract help than to chase away her grief. Neighbors come. Sô Manuel, like Vincente a drunk whose spirit has been trampled, sensing the urgency of the situation, calls for an ambulance which brings Vincente to a tuberculosis center in the city. He dies anonymously, for the death of an African is not of sufficient importance for a newspaper to mention his name; he is merely one of thirty-two unnamed "natives" who were reported dead on a particular day.

Mário António captures the flavor of life outside Luanda. The people who live in Môrro, carpenters, masons, washerwomen, all show concern for the misfortunes of Vincente and his family. The speech patterns of these poor people are faithfully reproduced: "Você" becomes "vucê" and "porquê" is "pruquê". Verbs are at times not conjugated correctly as when Sá Domingas comments "Nos não ganha para comer" (We no earn to live). Like Luandino Vieira, Mário António in "O Cozinhiero Vincente" recreates the language actually spoken by the people he writes about.

But the spirit of Europe which seduced the poet inevitably captured the imagination of the short story writer as well. The stories become more and more complex, more and more subjective. Perhaps Mário António's most hermetic prose work is *Farra no Fim de Semana* (Weekend Binge). In this collection of short stories all but the initial story bears the name of a character in that story. For Mário António, a character is not defined by his actions, but rather by his thoughts, expressions and feelings which frequently he himself cannot fully understand. Often there are conflicting instincts that are resolved through a reconciliation of the self with the world, but often one feels such harmony is momentary and will pass before the character is fully aware of its very existence. Peace with the world, or "o desejado ultimo é não ter mais desejos" (the ultimate wish is to have no more wishes), is precarious, transitory. Characters seldom interact in these stories; in fact, generally they do just the opposite—they remain isolated from one another simply because each man inhabits a private universe that cannot be shared by another. At times, a character can recognize a kindred spirit, but beyond this recognition there are limits which keep each man a prisoner within himself. Alienation, the lucidity of the intellectual who, like Paul Valéry, finds that part of the self is unknowable, a quest for meaning in a gratuitous universe in which normal, sterile social congress cannot suffice, the complexity of individual lives—these are among the principal themes of *Farra no Fim de Semana*.

Mário António's characters seek and often find Sartrean "moments privilégiés," moments when the mind ceases its incessant hunt and lets itself be absorbed into the physical and spiritual world—at times the face, hand or gesture of a woman provokes a moment of epiphany; or in three of the stories, this moment arises through contact with waves washing the shore to tell a character that he is pure, that he is part of an eternal rhythm of water and land.

It is only the intellectual who is sufficiently aware of his isolation and of the possibility of integrating the self into the world of man and beyond, but such integration can only be effected through a stultification of conscious experience, through an unconscious abandoning of the self to the world. In other words, the intellect that perceives must be killed for total perception to be realized.

In most of these stories setting matters little, for the central stage is the mind of the character. However, in "Avó Maria" Mário António successfully uses an African backdrop to give the story a particularly African flavor. Manuel, an unhappy and frequently depressed young man, given to long periods of withdrawal from his family from whom he feels alienated, has always been a source of grief to Avó Maria (grandmother Maria) as well as to his wife, Mariana. Avó Maria is not, in fact, his grandmother; she is his great aunt. When he was a small boy, she took charge of him and became his:

Avó dos cuidados da sua infância em perigo, a da vigilância das forças ocultas que o ameaçavam, a dos esforços para a sua integração num mundo que ele sentia . . . não ser aquele em que poderia viver . . .[15]

grandmother protecting him from the cares of his endangered childhood, the grandmother of vigilance against occult forces that were threatening him, the grandmother of those forces working for his integration into a world that he felt he could not live in.

We are not told what specific problems confronted Manuel, but the allusions to "occult forces" and an "endangered childhood" suggest that evil forces were at work to harm him. Perhaps he was a twin; perhaps his family had been cursed; perhaps, like Shaka Zulu, he was illegitimate and an object of ridicule to other children—certainly Mário António implies that certain hostile elements within a specifically African community were present. To combat these potentially destructive forces, Avó Maria uses magic of her own (she once saved him from evil forces through the intervention of Our Lady of the Rosary, who comes to her in a dream). But that alone is not sufficient. Manuel must learn that he is not alone, that there is an enormous web that encompasses and unites all men with each other, the world, and beyond. Avó Maria, as an African woman, knows that Manuel's solitude is alien to the cultural values of his society. African societies are communal. The African has traditionally believed in an integrated world in which the living, their ancestors, and plants and animals interact with one another. The physical world and the spiritual world commune with one another; there is nothing that does not belong.

Mário António uses various techniques to present this African world in "Avó Maria." The title of the story suggests that Avó Maria, not Manuel, is the principal figure and reinforces the idea that her position is the dominant one in the story. The story begins and closes with an image of the branches of the mulemba tree. This circular image further suggests an ordered universe in which everything belongs, including tribal religion and Christianity. The use of Kimbundu vocabulary serves further to bring us into a particular African world.

We do not know if Manuel will be reintegrated into his society. But he has come to think that perhaps Avó Maria is right:

Talvez houvesse um sentido naquilo tudo, pensava.[16]

Perhaps there was some sense to all that, he thought.

What is unique in this story in *Farra no Fim de Semana* is the traditional African view that the individual is by definition a member of a society that values integration above all else and that for the African, society is not an enemy that threatens the identity of the individual but rather a means of reconciling the individual with the world. In the other six stories in this collection, Africa does not play an essential role. At times one does not know if the characters are African. What is certain in these stories is that the alienated individual cannot depend on his society to help him establish a good relationship with his environment. This is an essentially European "weltanschauung" and contrasts markedly with the African philosophy as expressed in "Avó Maria."

* * * *

Even though the stories in *Crónica Da Cidade Estranha* (Chronicle of a Strange City), published by Agência Geral do Ultramar in 1964, are set in and around Luanda, they too, in general, lack a particularly Angolan or African dimension. The characters are alienated from their environment, from each other, and from themselves. Frequently they remember the vitality in the city before the faceless monsters of modern architecture, "aquela indiferença vertical de cimento armado" (that vertical indifference of armed cement), like an occupying army, destroyed a way of life. Natural smells, dirt roads, the quiet dignity of human contact, have been replaced by purifying deodorants, modern streets and vulgar night life. In his portrait of Luanda, however, Mário António could very well be writing about almost any modern city. His theme of isolation is again rooted in the West.

There are two parts to *Crónica da Cidade Estranha*: the first, written by M. António, contains fifteen portraits of alienated people; the second part, "Apendice," written by his friend Mário A. is divided into ten short segments. In the initial part, the author is detached; he is an objective spectator. The style is impersonal. We are far from the Luanda of *Luuanda* in which Luandino identifies with the people of the musseque. Mário António, through his characters, is actually expressing his own alienation. This is done more directly in the second part; the much shorter "chapters" permit a more condensed and concentrated vision. Here are snapshots in an album of memories. Nevertheless, despite the differences in style, the decision to write under two names is not much more than a clever stunt. My guess is that the two parts were written at different times.

When a character is recapturing memories of smells or clouds or vegetation, the series of images flash by without demarcation. A sentence of a hundred words is quite common and there are sentences of well over two hundred words. One is reminded of Proust's syntactic constructions. But Luanda is not Illiers. Mário António's people are poor; they live in crowded conditions. Frequently without jobs and without hope, they can

Modern Luanda along the sea.

only perceive the misery of their lives. But their alienation cannot be expressed because in the world of Mário António language is an inadequate means of communication. For instance, in "Passeio de Barco" (Boat Trip) Zeca cannot tell Mário that their friendship is impure, that Zeca resents the freedom and spontaneity of his schoolmates. Surely the ethos of silence is not absolute and Zeca's withdrawal into himself accomplishes little.

If total communication between people is impossible, significant communication is not. The fact that modern writers from Europe and the United States frequently speak of a world in which man is alienated does not at all mean that such a world is universal. The isolation of modern Western man is a by-product of specific historic and social phenomena: the loss of Christian faith, the advent of technology, particularly as it provides for individual mobility, the nature of bourgeois society, two world wars that shattered the West's image of itself as the apex of human civilization. Africa has its own problems. These are the problems of countries that need to develop or are presently developing modern technologies, countries that are emerging from a colonial past into an unpredictable future. Poverty, illiteracy, poor health facilities, corrupt government, and perhaps most of all a need to recapture confidence based on pride in one's own cultural heritage—these are among Africa's problems. Mário António, like Ayi Kwei Armah of Ghana in his novels, and Lenrie Peters of Gambia, in *The Second Round*, is doing a disservice to Africa by importing the face of Europe, a face of despair and alienation into an African environment and claiming that the European model is African. Mário António would have been more reflective of his zeitgeist had he set his *Crónica* in Lisbon, Marseilles or Detroit.

* * * *

The publication of *Mahezu* in 1966, one year after that of *Farra No Fim de Semana* and just two years after *Crónica da Cidade Estranha* marks for Mário António a literary homecoming. Europe does not exist in these six stories inspired by traditional oral tales that reflect the wisdom of Africa. Mário António recalls that his grandmother used to tell him such stories, but all that has remained in his memory are the general feelings these stories aroused. Like nearly all of Angola's urban educated people, he lost direct contact with his Kimbundu heritage; only through reading such books as Chatelian's *Contos Populares de Angola* (Popular Tales of Angola), Ennig's *Umbundo Folk Tales from Angola* and *I Contribuição para o estudo crítico da bibliografia de conto popular das Etnias Angolanas* (A Contribution towards a Critical Study of the Bibliography of Ethnic Angolan Popular Tales) of Lopes Cardoso could Mário António come to know the richness and variety of the oral literature of Angola.

"Mahezu" is a Kimbundu word spoken by the story teller when he has concluded his tale. It means "the end"—it is time for the listener to make of the tale what he will. *Mahezu* is a work of fiction; the inspiration is African, but Mário António is not recreating familiar oral literature. Rather he composes his own plots. There are trickster tales, moral fables and myths. Animals, human and supernatural creatures interact. Those familiar with the romantic world of the Yoruba writer, Amos Tutuola, will not be surprised to read of the innocent girl made prisoner by a multi-headed monster who takes her through an invisible entrance to his home among the palisades. No complete gentleman, this fellow! She is saved by a young boy who, turning himself into a bird, penetrates the monster's den and subsequently kills him by stuffing his many mouths with rocks.

The tortoise is a principal character. In one of the more intriguing narratives, the tortoise convinces his friend the dog that they should dine on one of the four leopard cubs that Mr. Dog guards for Madam Leopard. Explaining that the mother will not know that a cub is missing since she feeds them individually, Mr. Tortoise assuages his host's fears. Nature being what it is, Mr. Tortoise returns on several occasions to feast on the second and third cubs of Madam Leopard. Mr. Tortoise and Mr. Dog have eaten well, but the latter fears that the mother will notice that instead of bringing four cubs to be fed, the dog has brought the same cub four times. Sure enough, Madam Leopard grows suspicious and announces to Mr. Dog that tomorrow she wishes the four cubs to be brought to her together so she can play with them. Frightened and trembling, Mr. Dog relates his plight to Mr. Tortoise. No problem, says the wily tortoise—let's enjoy the fourth cub. Incredulous, Mr. Dog looks bewildered, but he is relieved upon hearing his friend's plan to save his life. The next day when Madam Leopard asks for her cubs, their canine guardian tells her she will find them inside the cave, after which he dashes towards the home of Mr. Man, screaming that a leopard is on the way to attack him. Grateful for the warning, Man protects the dog, giving him bones and other food as well. Mr. Dog, learning from his past errors, will be loyal to his new master.

In a more philosophic tale "Um Pequeno, um Grande Chefe" (A Small, A Great Chief), a small chief who has sworn allegiance to a greater chief is accused unjustly of betrayal. The faithful and wise small chief proclaims his innocence, but the powerful chief, unwilling to listen to reason, orders that a new pledge be sworn. The lesser chief prefers death, for a second pledge would mean that the first pledge had been violated. This honest man and his loyal counselors are to be put to death as traitors. Mário António does not tell us who has betrayed the small chief to the greater chief, but certainly evil forces are at work. The blindness of the powerful chief, his trust in those who deceive him—surely these are dangerous qualities in a leader; and the death of the small chief is a tragedy; his unwavering fidelity to his superior and to truth make him a figure worthy of admiration.

That Mário António returns to Angolan traditions in his prose indicates that in leaving Africa, Africa has not completely left him. His innumerable scholarly essays on Angolan and Lusophone African literature and culture are further evidence of his involvement with African traditions. Still there is the feeling that Mário António is struggling to recapture something that he has lost. Like those European intellectuals whose works in part inspired the writing of *Mahezu*, Mário António is in a way, a foreigner. "Mestiço", in the case of Mário António, is not a happy resolution of two cultures, but an alienation from both. Like the girl in his tale, "Lago" (Lake), who witnessed from a hill the destruction by drowning of the people in her village, Mário António cannot return to the communal security of an African past that for him, at least, is irretrievable.

Footnotes

1. My italics.

2. Mário António, Preface to *Poetas Angolanos*, edit. Carlos Eduardo, (Lisbon, Casa dos Estudantes do Império, 1959).

3. Mário António, *100 Poemas* (Luanda, ABC, 1963), pp. 8-10.

4. *Ibid*, p. 12.

5. *Ibid*, p. 34.

6. *Ibid*, p. 55.

7. *Ibid*, p. 77.

8. *Ibid*, p. 162.

9. Mário António, *Farra no Fim de Semana* (Braga, Editora Pax, 1965), pp. 105-106.

10. Mário António, *Rosto de Europa* (Braga, Editora Pax, 1968), p. 54.

11. *Ibid*, pp. 68-69.

12. Chinua Achebe points out in two illuminating essays entitled "Colonialist Criticism" and "Thoughts on the African Novel," that Western and African literary critics, who have been seduced by the idea that African literature to be a valid literature should go beyond regionalism to universality, are voicing a prejudice inspired by Western criteria. To assert that African literature rooted in African society is merely "regional" while literature rooted in Western values is "universal" is to accept the myth that universal truth is the sole property of the West.

13. Mário António, "O Cozinhiero Vincente" in Fernando Mourão, *Contistas Angolanos* (Lisbon, Casa dos Estudantes do Império, 1960), p. 74.

14. *Ibid*, p. 76.

15. *Farra no Fim de Semana*, pp. 81-82.

16. *Ibid*, p. 85.

BALTASAR LOPES AND THE MORNA OF CAPE VERDE

The islands of Cape Verde are most inhospitable to man. Since the discovery of the islands over five centuries ago, repeated droughts, some of them lasting several years, have wiped out sizeable elements of the population. Starvation, poverty and sickness have become a way of life. Because life is difficult, many Cape Verdeans have chosen to emigrate to North Africa, to Argentina, to Portugal—to any place where they can earn enough money to live a dignified life with sufficient comfort. The history of Cape Verde is a horribly monotonous pattern of insufficient rain and insufficient livelihood which produces inevitable sufferings.

Yet these islands constitute one of man's most praiseworthy achievements: "O mais completo exemplo de harmonia racial que o mundo já conheceu" (The most perfect example of racial harmony that the world has yet known) in the words of Manuel Ferreira.[1] There were no native Cape Verdeans when Portuguese explorers first set foot on the islands; the present Crioulo population is over two-thirds mulatto "mestiço na cor e mestiço na cultura"[2] (mulatto in color and mulatto in culture), a direct result of the interaction of Portuguese whites and black slaves brought primarily from Guinea centuries ago. The Cape Verdean phenomenon refutes the theory expressed by many, including Aimé Césaire, that a harmonious non-racial culture cannot result from the meeting of European and African peoples.

Perhaps Cape Verde's most celebrated mulatto is Baltasar Lopes. He was born in the town of Ribeira Brava on the island of São Nicolau on April 23, 1907. Lopes earned degrees from the Faculties of Law and Letters of the University of Lisbon. However, in the thirties, after having spent several years teaching in Portugal, Baltasar Lopes returned to Cape

Verde as a teacher at the Liceu Gil Eanes on the island of São Vincente. A director of the school for many years, he retired in 1972. Lopes turned down an offer in 1945 to be a professor at the Faculty of Letters at the University of Lisbon. He chose rather to spend his life working on Cape Verde, for he must have felt that he could contribute more to his society by teaching at the secondary level than by gaining a prestigious position in a major European university. When, in 1973, I first came to Portugal, I met several Cape Verdean students living in Coimbra; I remember one girl who spoke with pride of having had Baltasar Lopes as a teacher. Since there are not many secondary schools in Cape Verde, many of the students who have continued their education have had the good fortune to study under a major African literary figure.

As a poet, short story writer, novelist, philologist and essayist, Baltasar Lopes is one of the prime movers of modern Cape Verdean literature. In 1936, along with Jorge Barbosa and Manuel Lopes, he gave birth to the first issue of *Claridade*, a journal whose main purpose was an examination of the Cape Verdean culture and a study of the roots of that culture.[3] *Claridade* was inspired by several sources—the modernist Portuguese literary journal *Presença* in which Fernando Pessoa, among others, challenged the insipid "fin de siècle" literature made otiose by a paltry imitation of the French; the Brazilian writers in the decade of the 30's, particularly José Lins de Rego, Jorge de Lima, Érico Veríssimo and Jorge Amado, who broke away from a purely Portuguese literature to create a modern fiction expressing the values, the language and the nature of Brazilian society; and most importantly, the conviction that the Cape Verdean writer must not only express his own "cabo-verdeanidade," but also that he is obliged to protest the economic conditions endured by the poor people who inhabit Cape Verde. *Claridade* was a clarion call for revitalization of a Cape Verdean literature that indeed had existed since the sixteenth century, but with a new emphasis on the Crioulo culture that had evolved. In fact, in two of the first three issues, poems written in Crioulo appeared on the cover.[4]

Lopes has contributed stories and poems to *Claridade* as well as to other journals including *Atlântico, Vértice, Colóquio, Cabo Verde* and *Mensagem*. As a poet, he has written under the pseudonym Osvaldo Alcântara. Lopes' poetry spans five decades. Like Senghor, he celebrates the mother, but for Lopes the African mother—the African soul of Cape Verde—is not luxuriant and sensual; it is frequently without life. In "Mamãe" Lopes, the son, sings a song of love for his suffering mother:

> Mamãezinha
> eu queria dizir minha oração
> mas não posso:
> minha oracão adormece

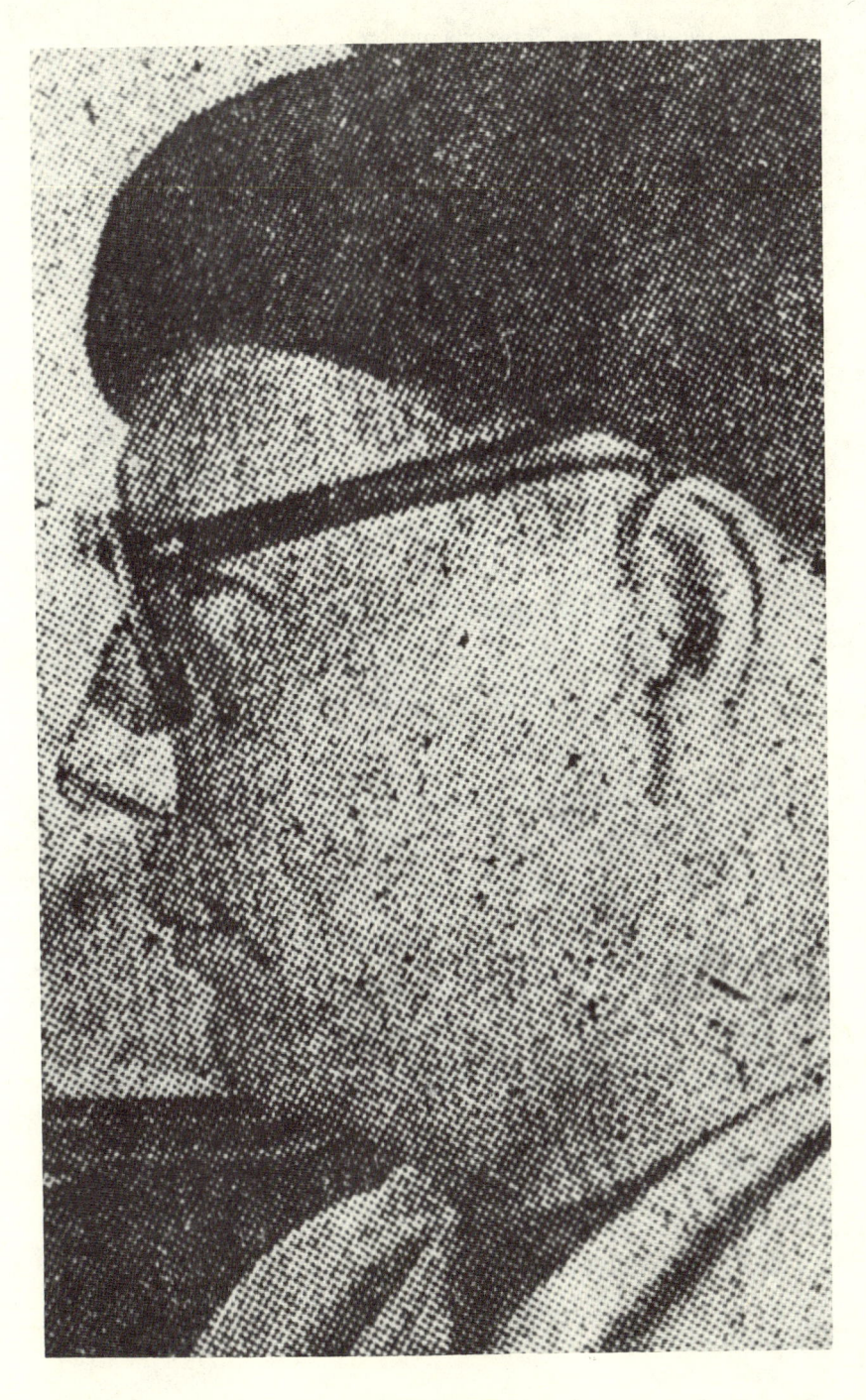

Baltasar Lopes

> nos meus olhos, que choram a tua dor
> de nos quereres alimentar
> a não poderes.

> Mother dear
> I wanted to say my prayer
> but I cannot:
> my prayer sleeps
> in my eyes, which cry for your grief
> of wanting to nourish us
> but being unable to do so.

She has been reported dead, buried in a shroud of rain, but the son refuses to accept her death:

> Não morreste, não Mamãezinha?
> Estás apenas adormecida
> para amanhã te levantares. . .
> Amanhã, quando saires,
> eu pegarei o balaio
> e irei atrás de ti. . .
> E eu me alimentarei do teu imenso carinho. . .[5]

> No, you didn't die, Mother dear?
> You are only sleeping
> in order to awaken tomorrow. . .
> Tomorrow, when you go out
> I will take the straw basket
> and will follow you. . .
> And I will nourish myself in your immense kindness. . . .

The theme of rebirth, of a continuation of a process of life from a distant past into an unfathomable future is a theme that reoccurs in such poems as "Presença", published in 1936 and "Mar" (Sea) published in 1973. In "Presença" Mamãezinha inspires:

> O lirismo antigo da minha raça
> crucificada
> na encruzilhada
> de duas sensibilidades. . . .[6]

> The ancient lyricism of my race
> crucified
> at the crossway
> of two sensibilities. . . .

Cover of *Claridade* magazine.

Crucified not by the white man as is Senghor's Chaka but by unfriendly nature. There is death, but there is also life:

> nesta minha terra de torturadas esperanças
> que morrem todos os dias—
> e nunca morrem
> porque cada dia ressuscitam
> na aldeia perpetuadora
> dos teus beijos.[7]

> in this land of tortured hopes
> which die every day—
> and never die
> because each day they are reborn
> in the perpetual village
> of your kisses.

Still there is the sea to offer visions of new adventures and unattainable dreams, so the poet-speaker can look to the future:

> Eu sou o cavaleiro moço
> que todos os dias parte em cruzada
> para as miragens dos poentes do mar. . . .[8]

> I am the boy-knight
> who each day embarks on a crusade
> for the mirages of sunsets at sea. . . .

The sea is a principal theme of Cape Verdean poetry. Jorge Barbosa in "Poemas do Mar" (Poems of the Sea), Arnaldo França in "Dois Poemas do Mar" (Two Poems of the Sea), and Manual Lopes in "Naufrágio" (Shipwreck) speak of the Atlantic that can take a man to a new life or to his death. In Baltasar Lopes' poem, "Mar" (Sea), the sea is a symbol of all that is mysterious and of all that endures. It is a waterless ocean; it is a saltless ocean; it is a mysterious ocean:

> no mar sem águas, no mar
> com águas sem sal que vêm a deluir-se
> lá do fundo das distâncias mágicas![9]

> in the sea without waters in the sea
> with waters but without salt which comes to be diluted
> there from the depth of magical distances!

The poetry of Baltasar Lopes has been anthologized in various collections of Cape Verdean and Lusophone African writings. Nevertheless, it is as a writer of prose that Lopes is most at home, for he can treat in far greater detail the characters and the land that he knows and loves.

* * * *

Lopes' first and only novel, *Chiquinho,* was first published in 1947. A second edition appeared in 1961. To appreciate the impact of *Chiquinho,* one must realize that it is to the literature of Cape Verde what *Things Fall Apart* is to Nigerian fiction and *L'Enfant Noir* is to Francophone African prose. Moreover, Lopes' novel was written a decade before the appearance of the two above mentioned pivotal works in African fiction. In his novel Lopes succeeds in portraying the lives of ordinary and extraordinary people, old and young, rebellious and timid, complex and simple, who struggle to survive in the terraqueous world which is Cape Verde. Within *Chiquinho* are found those literary themes that have been the hallmark of modern literature from this small Atlantic archipelago: drought, starvation, economic depression, "terra longismo" (emigration), the sea, social protest, a Crioulo saudade for a better life that has been dreamed of or that must be forged by man, solitude, music (especially the "morna"), and most important, an assertion of the values and traditions of the Cape Verdean people. It is a Crioulo world in which belief in orthodox Catholicism and stories of witchcraft are harmoniously blended, in which the waltz and batuque are danced. Parables, folk tales, myths and proverbs are recounted as sources of traditional wisdom and belief. Perhaps the most enchanting story concerns the mermaid of the sea, that beautiful eternal seductress, eternally young, eternally compassionate, who forever embraces dead sailors. The "moça do mar" never tires of showing her love for the Cape Verdean who will never return to his homeland. Although the novel is written in Portuguese, Crioulo dialect words and phrases appear from time to time to help bring us into the uniquely communal Cape Verdean culture whose image Lopes presents.

Chiquinho is written in three parts. In the first part, entitled "Infância" (Childhood), Chiquinho recounts the experiences of his early years. We are introduced to a variety of characters who in one way or another play a part in his life. His father, António Manuel, works in America in a cotton factory. His letters, gifts, and money sent from 102 South Second Street are always received with great joy. Without his money the family's life on the island of São Nicolau would undoubtedly be more difficult, for when the rains cease to provide needed water, those who can afford irrigation have a far better chance to survive. For the young Chiquinho, America is an extention of Cape Verde in which all the pleasant aspects of island life are magnified while the horrible aspects are nonexistent. He imagines his father living in a Cape Verdean house while women, cooking with Cape Verdean pots over a fire, prepare for him traditional Cape Verdean meals. His mother, hard working and severe, is a stern mistress within the home, but whenever children other than her own come with a problem, she offers them protection, warmth and encouragement.

Many of the thirty-one chapters in this initial part are character sketches or anecdotes. In one, Chiquinho's grandmother recalls the time when, as a small girl, she survived a cholera epidemic that was so devastating that the dying were often buried along with the dead in order to save digging separate graves for them the next day. In another, tio Joca, who spends his life lamenting his drinking bouts and fathering illegitimate children, recalls his days as a Latin student. His love of Virgil has never left him. When Chiquinho goes to stay with him when he attends school, tio Joca makes sure that his young disciple learns his lessons. Perhaps the saddest life is that of Toi Mulato who lives with his aged and cantankerous grandmother. She severely beats him when he returns from the store with only two of the three liters of milk that he was to purchase. Toi Mulato did not steal the milk, but his grandmother would never believe that he had given the milk to a very poor and sickly woman who needed it.

Toi Mulato, an outstanding student and a gentle boy, is the man of a family that treats him without appreciation. He rushes to see ships when they come in even though he knows that leaving his grandmother will bring him a certain beating. There is Nhô Chic Ana, married fifty years to Nhana Bonga. He went to sea, returned, and has remained a prisoner of the hoe, forever regretting that he abandoned a sailor's life. Chico Zepa, obstreperous and bold, listening to stories of America from Nhô João Joana, refuses to be a prisoner of the harvest. He has even learned some American words to impress his peers. For Chico each man makes his own destiny; to accept passively the bondage of Cape Verde is to accept misery. Bibia Ludovna is possessed of the evil spirit of António Carrinho. Witchcraft must be used to rescue her from a madness caused by her tormentor. A horrible story is told of José Capado whose jealous wife drugs him, castrates him, and then invites her husband's lover to see the product of her revenge. Each of these characters, each of these stories, combine to give Chiquinho an exposure to life's adventures and life's sadnesses. But it is not until the outbreak of World War I that Chiquinho realizes that his spontaneous non-involvement has died and that the world of responsibility and adulthood is before him. News comes of a death at sea and then there is his first exposure at age fourteen to serious hunger. Older people recall the drought of '96. Corn growers hold what corn they have to get a better price. Children die and the fortunate Chiquinho, with his fifth level of school behind him, plans to go to the island of São Vincente to continue his education.

Cover of *Chiquinho* by Baltasar Lopes.

But education means alienation, for with knowledge comes awareness and a new sensitivity that result in inevitable estrangement. This is a common theme in African literature. For instance, Camara Laye's "l'enfant noir' can never return to his integrated past once he has left it for the schools of Conakry and Paris. Chiquinho, in the second part of the novel "São Vincente" enters a new world where he is eighteen years old.

São Vincente does not turn out to be the romantic place that it was in the imagination of the youth of São Nicolau. Unemployment is rampant. The construction of a newer and larger port at Dakar has resulted in a major reduction in shipping traffic for São Vicente. Girls without work are at times lured to the cabarets of Dakar where they will dance in the smoke-filled rooms frequented by lecherous Frenchmen. Frequently they are unaware of the sordid life that awaits them on the continent. In order to attempt to remedy some of these problems, Chiquinho and a group of intellectual friends, led by Andrézinho, nicknamed "O Erudito" on account of his scholarly mind, seek to organize workers so that they can express their will as a strong, unified body; to establish on the island a port to compete with that of Dakar is a major priority. But the idealism and commitment of Andrézinho and his followers is not shared by many of the people, who are too indifferent or apathetic to bother about actively seeking a better way of life on the island and throughout Cape Verde. Andrézinho's group is called "o Gremio Cultural Cabo-Verdeano" (The Cultural Society of Cape Verde). Not only is he interested in improving the material lives of the laborers, but he is equally involved in a project to investigate the particular cultural and spiritual traditions of the Cape Verdean people throughout the world, for he believes that the future of Cape Verde must be built on an understanding and appreciation of those features that are unique to Cape Verdean culture. O Erudito believes that a knowledge of the history and literature of his people is a necessary step in the process of understanding the past. He even contemplates editing an anthology of popular Cape Verdean literature.

Chiquinho lives with Andrézinho's family. His friend's father has emigrated to Argentina. His seventeen year old sister, Nuninha, interests Chiquinho as much if not more than her older brother. Their innocent love grows during the two years that Chiquinho spends in São Vincente. They speak of marriage and dream of a time when they can begin to build a life together.

Friendships are made with Manuel de Brito, the poorest boy in the sixth level class, nicknamed "Parafuso," for he is tall and extremely thin like the narrow trunk of a coconut palm. Parafuso, a Latin scholar, lives a life of noble endurance. His pride forbids him to accept money or food. He becomes very ill, for his unemployed father cannot provide sufficient means to feed his family decently. As his illness becomes worse, he misses many days of school. Worried about him, his friends contrive to keep him off the football team, for they realize that playing football would certainly be detrimental to his health. A doctor asserts that Parafuso is tubercular, that he needs good food and a long period of rest in a different climate. The poverty of his family condemns him. His friends do their best; to spare his dignity, they plot with his father who pretends that the money given by all the boys to purchase eggs and meat for Parafuso has been earned from a newly found job. But moral resistance cannot save a decaying body. Parafuso dies. The hope of his family dies. It is now his younger brother who must go to school to find a way to bring a better life for them.

Nonó, the lyric poet of the group, composes Crioulo "mornas." The morna of Cape Verde is usually a sad song expressing the collective grief of the people through a single voice that speaks of individual suffering. It is somewhat akin to the fado of Portugal or the lament of Corsica. In the words of Jorge Barbosa:

> A Morna. . .
> parece que é o eco en tua alma
> da voz do Mar
> e da nostalgia das terras mais ao longe
> que o Mar te confida
> o eco
>   da voz da chuva desejada,
> o eco
>   da voz interior de nós todos,
>   da voz da mossa tragédia sem eco!
>
> A Morna. . .
> tem de ti e das coisas que nos rodeiam
> a expressão da nossa humildade,
> a expressão passiva do nosso drama
> da nossa revolta,
>   da nossa silenciosa revolta melancólica![10]

> The Morna. . .
> it seems that it is the echo in your soul
> of the voice of the Sea
> and of the nostalgia of lands farther away
> the Sea invites you
> the echo
>   of the voice of desired rain,
> the echo
>   of the interior voice of all of us,
>   of the voice of our tragedy without echo!

> The Morna...
> takes from you and the things that surround us
> the expression of our humility
> the passive expression of our drama
> of our revolt,
> >of our silent melancholy revolt!

During carnival in which there are spirited musical contests among different groups, one playing jazz, another playing the sensual music of the batuque, various mornas are sung. Nonó, accompanied by guitar, sings the following Crioulo composition:

> Na sê campo simiado di strela
> Nhor Dê ficha Didinha Lua
> na tumba di nôte sucuro...
> Mochinhos de Cabo Verde,
> jâ nhôs ficâ sim madrinha
> pamôdi Nhor Des di Céu
> jâ fichá Didinha Lua
> na tumba di nôte sucuro...[11]

Nonó's mornas linger in the mind of Chiquinho. He likes, in particular, the morna about love and the incomparable sweetness expressed in the black eyes of a Crioulo woman, for being in love himself, he responds to the personal and immediate impact of the words.

Chiquinho tries his hand at writing. The result is a romantic novel, *As Núpcias do Príncipe Siddhartha* (The Nuptuals of Prince Siddhartha), in which the oriental hero rejects the beautiful Yasodhara to devote himself to his religious calling. Perhaps Lopes is poking fun at the Cape Verdean writer who might choose to seek inspiration in the romantic realm of a foreign past rather than in his own traditional culture. Perhaps the novel is a mere reflection of Chiquinho's idealized, romantic vision. In any case it is a puerile work that is antithetical in style, tone and temperament to the novel *Chiquinho*.

The third part of Lopes' story is called "Ás-Águas" (The Waters). Having completed his two year academic program at São Vincente, Chiquinho returns to São Nicholau but finds that he is a stranger. The idealized world of childhood has been destroyed by his perception of suffering and struggle. Moreover he no longer blindly adheres to the memorized wisdom of many older folk on the island, often eager to advise him. He frequently thinks of his school friends with whom he communicated on a serious and personal level. Still, there are a few people whose intellectual natures provide him with stimulating conversation. One such is Sr. Euclides Varanda, an eccentric recluse devoted to mysticism, literature, and at times Gaida,

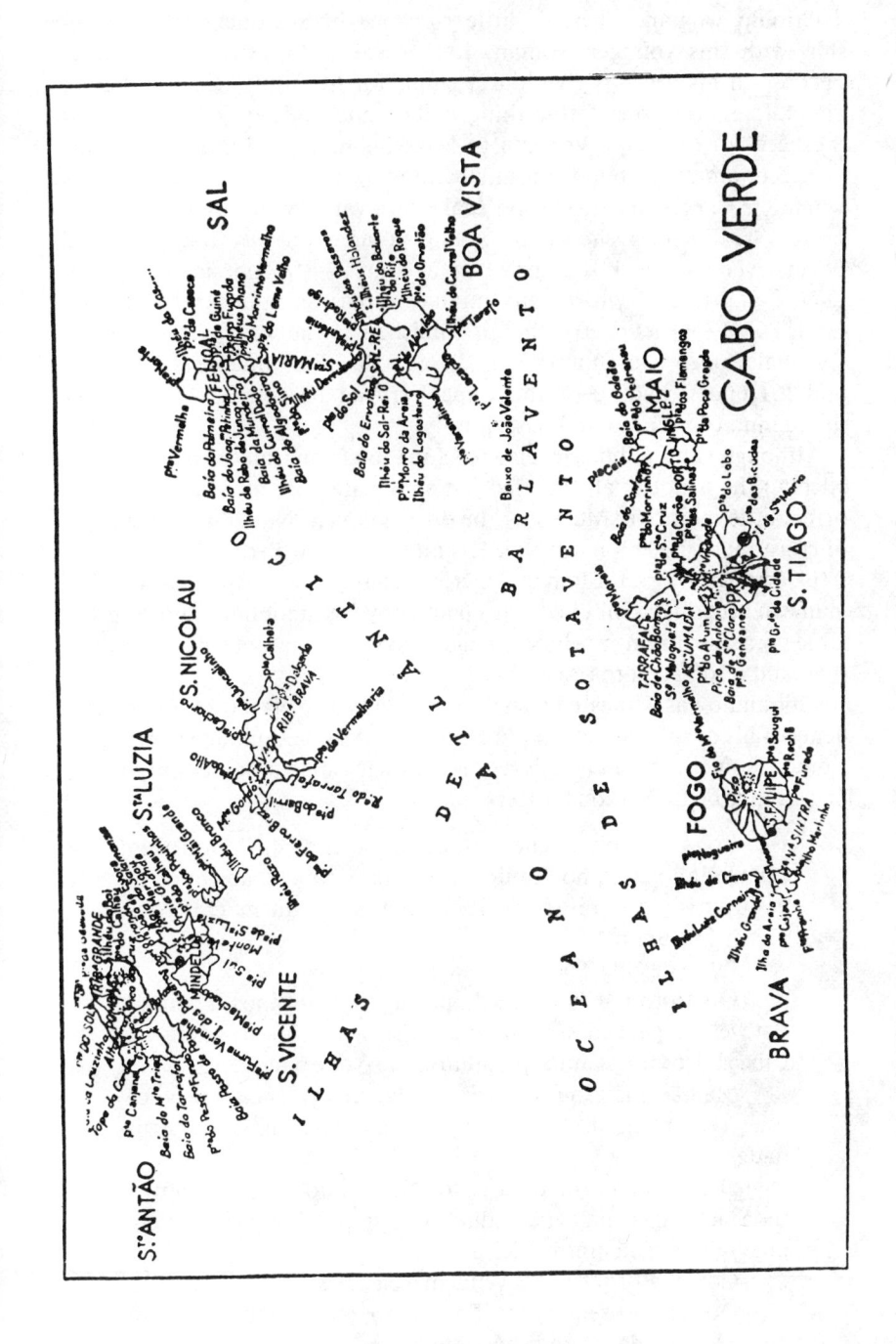

Map of Cape Verde.

a Crioulo woman. There is little romance in Sr. Euclides' relationship with this younger woman. Rather she is to serve one essential purpose in his life—to give him a child, for he firmly believes that to die childless is a lamentable thing. Chiquinho and his friend speak of the need for the Cape Verdean to leave his homeland in order to survive economically, but without abandoning the soul of Cape Verde, which is necessary for spiritual survival. With understandable pride, Sr. Euclides shows his young companion his first published poems which earned first prize in a contest—"A poesia que publiquei é a primeira vitória das minhas forças spirituais sobre a matéria. . . ."[12] (The poetry that I published is the first victory of my spiritual forces over matter. . . ."). Sr. Euclides' intense seriousness and his understanding of the Cape Verdean need to create a better life remind Chiquinho of Andrézinho.

Although Chiquinho is given a teaching job in an isolated place on São Nicolau, he is not at all satisfied; an anticipated life of relative poverty offers little incentive. Moreover, he does not want Nuninha to live a life of constant struggle for survival. His father, in New Bedford, Massachusetts, arranges work for him in America. The appeal of America, where a man can get a high school education and buy a gramophone and comfortable home furnishings, where a steady income is guaranteed—the call of that land is too great to resist.

Chiquinho has witnessed a terrible drought since his return home. Students of his die of starvation; old Nhô Chic' Ana dies; unnamed men and women, some with small children, leave their isolated homes only to die in a strange bed. Everyone suffers:

> Logo cedinho, chegou-nos à soleira da porta um rapazotinho de olhos timídos. Trazia à cabeça um objecto embrulhado em restos de saco. Perguntei quem era. Mamãe informou-me:
> Filho de Nhá Tuda Aninha.
> O garoto parou ao pé da porta, com os olhos no chão. Esteve um pedaço sem dizer ao que ia, o objecto ainda na cabeça. Por fim mamãe perguntou-lhe o que queria.
> Mamãe mandou-me trazer esta conveniência, se você quer comrar. Diz que é para socorrer uma necessidade. . .
> Depôs na porta o objecto. Seus olhos acentuavam a reticência das palavras, ditas em tom de quem receia uma recusa. Era uma caldeira.
> Come? Porquê vocês vendem a caldeira?
> Dormimos sem cear, Totoninho está doente, está só pedindo comida, mamãe não tem. . .

Perguntei-lhe quantos irmãos eram.
Vivemos seis com mamãe. Totoninho é o codê, está só a pedir comida, não dormiu chorando fome, fome dói. . .
Mas vocês vendem a caldeira porquê? Podiam vender outra coisa. . .
Não temos mais nada. Mamãe já vendeu o vestido novo que tinha, e tresantontem fomos à vila vender a cama para lenha.
Mas foram buscar a ração na Irmandade. . .
Disseram que não tinha mais. Não chegou para todo o mundo. Eu bem que pedi, porque Totoninho está doente, mas no fim tive de vir sem nada. . .
Tua mãe não foi para lenha?
Mamãe não pode, está pele e osso, tem um ror te dias não comemos comida da caldeira. Ontem só teve chá amargoso de folha de laranjeira. Mamãe cozeu miolo de troco de babaneira e a gente comeu. Totoninho está muito fraço, a gente tem fome, mamãe está só a chorar. . .
Mamãe deu- lhe café a uma racha de cuscuz. Mas o garoto só bebeu o café, não comeu o cuscuz.
Por que não comes o cuscuz?
Para levar para Totoninho. . .[13]

Later, very early, a boy with timid eyes arrived at our doorstep. On his head he was carrying an unidentifiable object in the remains of what must once have been a sack. I asked him who he was. Mamãe informed me:
The son of Nhâ Tuda Aninha.
The lad stopped before the door, with downcast eyes. He waited a little while saying nothing, the thing still on his head. Finally mamãe asked him what he wanted.
Mamma asked me to bring this to you to see if you wished to buy it. She says it is to help us at this critical time. . .
He deposited the object at the door. His eyes reinforced the reticence of his words, spoken in a tone of one who fears a refusal. It was a kettle.
What? Why are you selling a kettle?
We went to bed without eating. Totoninho is sick, all he asks for is food, mamma doesn't have. . .
I asked him how many brothers and sisters he had.

Six of us are living with mother. Totoninho is the youngest, all he does is ask for food, he didn't sleep from crying from hunger...

But why are you selling the kettle? You could sell something else...

We have nothing. Mamma already sold her new dress and four days ago, we went into town to sell our bed for firewood.

But didn't you go for free food provided at the Irmandade...

They said they didn't have any more. There wasn't sufficient for everyone. It was I who asked, for Totoninho is sick, but in the end I had to return home with nothing...

Didn't your mother go for firewood?

Mamma can't, she is all skin and bones, for a long time we haven't eaten out of the kettle. Yesterday I only ate bitter tea made from orange leaves and Mamma cooked bits from a banana plant and we ate that. Totoninho is very weak, everyone is hungry, all mother does is cry...

Mamae gave him coffee and a serving of couscous. But the boy only drank the coffee; he didn't eat the couscous.

Why don't you eat the couscous?

It's for Totoninho...

The gray land provides food only for hordes of invading locusts. Chiquinho has heard that in the past such devastation caused by lack of rain has plagued the defenseless Cape Verdean people. His personal contact with famine reinforces his awareness that the soil of Cape Verde cannot adequately nourish either his body or his dreams. The last word in *Chiquinho* is "América," an ambivalent symbol, for only in emigration, in "terra longismo," can the Cape Verdean, who loves his homeland, find a means to support his family.

Although *Chiquinho* is not an autobiographical novel as such, different aspects of Baltasar Lopes' life can be seen in at least three characters—Chiquinho, Andrézinho and Euclides Varanda. Like Chiquinho, Lopes was born on the island of São Nicolou and later went to school in São Vincente. Moreoever, his protagonist's interest in writing a novel and composing poetry reflects the author's own literary inclinations. That Chiquinho works as a teacher in Cape Verde is a further point of similarity between the character and his creator. But it is the young Andrézinho and the old Euclides Varanda whose dedication to Cape Verdean culture and society echoes Lopes' own lifelong commitment to literature and social progress. Like Andrézinho, Lopes chose to spend his life working among his people. As a lawyer, Lopes has at times defended the rights of the weak and the poor in legal cases; he did, in fact, start a journal of Cape Verdean literature, *Claridade*, and thirteen years after the first publication of *Chiquinho*, he collected and edited the *Antologia da Ficcão Cabo-Verdiana Contemporânea* which Andrézinho had planned to do sometime in the future. Sr. Euclides is, in part, perhaps a portrait of Lopes' vision of himself as an old man—fiercely independent, proud of his literary accomplishments, and helpful to young Cape Verdians like Chiquinho who can profit from his experience and perceptions.

Certainly each of these characters comes to see the inherent tragedy of life on Cape Verde, the tragedy of a land continually ravaged by starvation where day to day living is frequently an assertion of human courage and dignity. *Chiquinho* is an extended morna;[14] the entire novel echoes the lines of Jorge Barbosa:

Morna
desassossego,
    voz
da nossa gente
reflexo subconsciente
    em nós
das vagas ao longo das praias;
    das aragens
que trazem um sorriso bom
    às equipagens
dos barquinhos à vela
e flexibilidades graciosas
    às folhagens
do milharal
musicanda rapsodias em surdina
nos tectos das casas pobres. . . .[15]

Disquieting Morna,
    voice
of our people
subconscious reflection
    in us
of the waves along the beaches;
    of the breezes
that bring a good smile

>   to the crews
>   of the small sailing boats
>   and graceful flexibilities
>   to the leaves
>   of the maize field
>   silently composing rhapsodies
>   in the ceilings of poor houses. . . .

* * * *

In 1960, exactly five hundred years after the discovery of Cape Verde, Lopes edited, as noted, his remarkable anthology of twenty-three Cape Verdean stories, *Antologia de Ficção Cabo-Verdiana Contemporânea*.[16] Nothing of this sort had ever been done before. Since the initial publication a quarter of a century earlier of *Claridade*, significant prose works had appeared from these Crioulo island whose total population numbers at present only 270,000. Manuel Lopes' novel, *Chuva Braba* (Savage Rain), the narratives of António Aurélio Gonçalves, "Pródiga" and "O enterro de nhâ Candinha Sena" (The Burial of Candinha Sena), and of course, *Chiquinho*, are ample evidence that an original and realistic regional Cape Verdean literature continued to grow.

Six of Lopes own stories appear in his anthology. Two of them, "Farafuso" and "Nhô Chic ' Ana," are chapter selections from *Chiquinho*; the other four were previously published in literary journals. "Dona Mana" and "Balanguinho" appeared in issues six and eight of *Claridade*; "A Caderneta" (The Pass) was first published in *Vértice* in January, 1949, while "Muminha vai para a escola" (Muminha Goes to School) came out in *Boletim Cabo Verde* in June, 1952. The theme of suffering pervades these stories. Muminha shoots himself through the mouth to end a life made miserable by epilepsy. It is not until the end of the story that we learn the nature of his sickness. The unnamed narrator recaptures the days in which he and Muminha were schoolmates. Muminha was not at all liked by his peers, for his wealth and his predilection for solitude set him apart. However, the boys slowly came to realize that their mysterious friend was not very different after all, that he, too, needed friendship and acceptance. With an awareness of his illness and its effect on his family, these boys came to regret their bullying tactics and to understand that suffering is not the sole property of the poor.

In "Dona Mana," "Balanguinho," and "A Caderneta" women are victims of erroneous judgment and bad fortune. Dona Mana, in her early forties, fights to keep the second of her three illegitimate children, each from a different father, but the court rules that she must give up her daughter to the father, who is better able to take care of her. Maria dos Réis, a former servant and friend of Dona Mana, tells the judge that Dona Mana was all but deserted by her parents when her first son, Candinho, was born. Left to herself, she had to rent rooms to seedy characters coming off the boats of Dakar. Her faith in God is her only security.

The woman narrator in "A Caderneta," seeking legal aid, tells a lawyer, "o senhor doutor," her story. No longer young and unable to earn a decent living, she has taken in a low class sailor. As a result of a complaint made against her by a group of younger women, who run their own particular center for visiting sailors, the poor lady is obliged to visit a hospital each week to be examined for venereal disease. She asks the lawyer for his help in rescinding the order requiring her to be inspected.

Women and children who suffer and know loneliness—this is the world of Baltasar Lopes' short stories. The women are too young to be close to death but too old to be attractive. Certainly the plight of these unfortunate characters, trapped in hopeless situations, cannot be remedied solely by legal means. What these women want is a restored sense of dignity and value. The disinterested study of their different psychological responses is one of Lopes' strengths. As a result he avoids sentimentality. Our pity is genuine because we recognize that each character who suffers is a distinct human being with particular virtues and vices. The stories are microcosmic portraits of the world of *Chiquinho* in which Cape Verde is a prison. However, unlike the men of *Chiquinho*, the women of the short stories have no chance to seek freedom in a land far from the isolated confines of the Crioulo world. They will live out their sad lives in anonymous degradation.

Footnotes

1. Manuel Ferreira, *No Reino de Caliban* (Lisbon, Seara Nova, 1975), p. xiv.

2. *Ibid,* p. 66.

3. In an essay "Consciencialização na Literature Caboverdiana" (Consciousness Raising in Cape-Verdian Literature), published in 1963, Onésimo Silveira argues that the Claridade Movement and the writers of its generation were inadequate and insufficient, for instead of being rooted in Cape Verdean culture as they were claiming, they were elitists, inspired by European traditions. Silveira claims that the "Nova Geração" (New Generation) of writers, in harmony with colleagues throughout Africa, is committed both to pointing out social and political problems and actively seeking solutions to these problems. But Silveira's attack on the Claridade generation is unwarranted. Their encouragement of Crioulo as a literary language, the communal ambiance established in the novels and stories, and the willingness to appreciate African as well as European contributions to Cape Verdean culture indicate that this literature was far from being Europeanized. Moreover, one must remember that great changes took place in Africa in the three decades between the first issue of *Claridade* and the publication of Silveira's essay. The young generation of African writers is obliged to seek its own way, but for it to deny the efficacy of the earlier generation who committed much of their work to social statement (albeit non-militant) would be to deny its literary tap roots.

4. There have been nine issues of *Claridade* published in Mindelo, São Vincente, from 1936 to 1960: 1936 - two issues; 1937 - one issue; 1947 - two issues; 1948, 1949, 1958, 1960 - one issued each year.

5. *No Reino de Caliban*, pp. 109-110.

6. *Ibid,* p. 111.

7. *Ibid,* p. 112.

8. *Ibid,* p. 112.

9. *Ibid,* p. 117.

10. Jorge Barbosa, "Irmão" (Brother) in *Ambiente,* 1941.

11. Baltasar Lopes, *Chiquinho,* third edition (Lisbon, Prelo Editora, 1970), p. 180. (The author has not offered an English version of the poem, for he does not feel "safe" working with the Crioulo text and he was unable to obtain an authoritative translation elsewhere. ED.)

12. *Ibid,* p. 230.

13. *Ibid,* pp. 276-277.

14. The morna is a unique expression of Cape Verde. It originated on the island of Boa Vista, whose mornas reflect the happy and elegant people who populate it. Each island not only has its own variety of Crioulo, but also has a particular tradition of the morna. On the island of Brava, the morna is a tearful song. The oldest morna on the island, "Brada-Maria," composed about 1830, still evokes weeping from listeners. Eugénio Tavares, the celebrated composer of mornas, came from Brava.

But the morna is not merely poetry put to music; it is dancing and gestures as well. Therefore, merely listening to a recording or reading a morna presents an incomplete picture. One must imagine dancers pressed tightly together, dancing as couples and nodding their heads as the orchestra plays and the singer chants. It is known that Tavares wrote the words, composed the music, and even danced to his own compositions with the beautiful girls of his land.

Much Cape Verdean music and literature is derived from the morna, for it is the consummate expression of the Cape Verdean spirit. Osório de Oliveiro in his essay, "Uma Poesia Ignorada," remarks that "Resume em sí todos os sentimentos e condensa todas as aspirações artististicas dos caboverdeanos." (It summarizes all the feelings and compresses all the artistic aspects of the people of Cape Verde.) It is in this sense that the novel *Chiquinho* can be seen figuratively as a morna, for it expresses the Crioulo affection "crecheu" and the rhythm of life on Cape Verde much as the mornas of old.

15. Jorge Barbosa, "Morna" in *Arquipélago,* 1935.

16. Included are stories by António Aurélio Gonçalves, Baltasar Lopes, Francisco Lopes, Gabriel Mariano, Jorge Barbosa, Henrique Teixeira da Sousa, Manuel Lopes, Pedro Duarte and Virgílio Avelino Pires.

LUÍS BERNARDO HONWANA AND LIVES OF HUMILIATION

Luís Bernardo Honwana of Mozambique has been ranked along side Baltasar Lopes and Luandino Vieira as a modern master of prose in Lusophone Africa even though he has published only one book, a collection of short stories, *Nós Matámos o CãoTinhoso* (We Killed Mangy-Dog). The son of Bernard Manuel, an interpreter employed by the Portuguese government in Moamba, and of Nelly Jeremias Nhaca, a domestic, Honwana, one of nine children, was born in Lourenço Marques (now called Maputo) in November, 1942. Until the age of seventeen he lived with his family in Moamba, a suburb or "caniço" of the capital. While completing his secondary education, Honwana worked as a journalist. In November, 1967, he was released from a political prison sentence, after which he went to Lisbon to study law. Presently, he is a secretary in the administration of Samora Machel.

Nós Matámos o Cão-Tinhoso was first published in 1964 by Publicações Tribuna in Lourenço Marques. Afrontamento in Portugal published a second edition in 1972 and a third edition has recently appeared in Mozambique. Dorothy Guedes' English translation of the stories was published in the African Writers Series by Heinemann in London in 1969. Several of Honwana's individual stories appeared originally in the newspaper *Noticias*; "Papá, Cobra e Eu" (Papa, Snake and I) was first published in English in *Modern African Prose* edited by the South African writer Richard Rive, and "As Mãos dos Pretos" (The Hands of the Blacks) appeared in *Black Orpheus* and later in Ulli Beier's *Political Spider and Other Stories*. London Magazine Edition in 1967 came out with the first English version of the title story; "Dina" appeared in English in Ezekiel Mphahlele's *African Writing Today*, also in 1967.

In his introduction to the first edition of *Nós Matámos o Cão-Tinhoso*

Honwana remarks, "Não sei se realmente sou escritor. . . Este livro de histórias é o testemunho em que tento retratar uma série de situações e procedimentos que talvez interesse conhecer." (I don't know if I really am a writer. . . This book of stories is a testimony in which I try to portray a series of situations and proceedings that perhaps might be of interest.)

The softness of tone and the tendency to understatement that are apparent in Honwana's modest confession are qualities that are also found in the stories. Although in relating the Mozambiquan experience under colonial rule in and around the caniços of Lourenco Marques, Honwana depicts the terrible humiliation of men and women and children as well as animals, he never raises his voice to scold. In fact, he seldom speaks directly of the fears, the isolation, the repressed hatred and the frustrations that his people face. Merely by presenting these people and their suffering, Honwana has succeeded as an artist in portraying the horrors of racism and economic exploitation that inevitably accompanied Portuguese colonial policy in Africa.

Toucinho, the narrator of "Nós Matámos o Cão-Tinhoso," is an innocent schoolboy. He is used to seeing Mangy-Dog looking at him with his enormous blue eyes as if he were asking for something. Mangy-Dog, his body emaciated, covered with scars and sores, trembling and swaying his head to and fro, would frequently spend hours at the school gate watching the other dogs playing and running and smelling each other. The other dogs showed little interest in Mangy-Dog; it was as if they, like most of the people, resented his pathetic condition. Only Isaura loved Mangy-Dog, but she was considered crazy. Isaura used to stroke the back of Mangy-Dog; she fed her friend part of her lunch and frequently spoke to him in a soft and sympathetic voice. Of course, she was teased by the other children who would make a circle around her shouting "Isaura-Cão-Tinhoso, Isaura-Cão-Tinhoso, Isaura-Cão-Tinhoso." There is a symbolic element in their taunting, for Isaura and Mangy-Dog are identified with one another. Both are pariahs; both suffer and both receive only scorn for their sentiments. Only Touchinho can penetrate their world, for he is able to empathize with them.

Toucinho realizes that Mangy-Dog is to die when he hears Senhor Administrador angrily comment that the dog should not be alive, that it is so rotten that it makes him feel sick. The white administrator has been losing at cards to the Veterinary Doctor; upon seeing Toucinho and Mangy-Dog, he spits at them, for of course he cannot spit and yell at the Veterinarian, the real source of his frustration. The weak man, to assert his importance, feels a need to dominate wherever he can. The victim is often defenseless, unable to resist an assault that he does not deserve. Mangy-Dog must die. Senhor Duarte of the Veterinary Department does not want to kill him himself, so he advises a group of boys including

Luís Bernardo Honwana

Toucinho that they might enjoy the good sport of using Mangy-Dog for target practice. The boys get guns and drag the sacrificial victim far from town. Only Toucinho admits that he is afraid, that he does not want to kill Mangy-Dog. But his manhood is attacked and in the end he joins the participants in the killing to prove that he is the equal of his peers. Toucinho must rationalize his act. He tells himself that Senhor Duarte has, in fact, ordered the boys to kill Mangy-Dog. Moreover, his sores wouldn't hurt him any more if he were dead. In addition, death would free the poor dog from the humiliation he endures at the hands of those boys in Standard I who throw stones at him and tease him. Toucinho further rationalizes that it wouldn't help to bring him home, to feed him well, to cure his sores, and to build a dog house for him, for perhaps Mangy-Dog would not like it. Throughout the story Toucinho repeatedly comments that Mangy-Dog would look at him like someone asking for something without wanting to say it. Toucinho does not perceive that, in fact, his canine friend really desires a home where he will be loved and cared for. Toucinho's rationalization that Mangy-Dog might not like a home is therefore both ironic and sad.

"Nós Matámos o Cão-Tinhoso" is not merely a story about a lonely dog and its unhappiness. It is a parable about an aspect of colonialism in Mozambique. The white administrators and Senhor Duarte are cowards as is Quim, the white leader of the gang of boys. To prove their superiority, their masculinity, these whites must destroy the weak, and in this story Mangy-Dog is identified with Isuara and at times Toucinho, neither of whom are white. The tragedy lies in the fact that Toucinho himself, more sensitive and compassionate than his friends, participates in the massacre of a creature he loves far more than he does any of his schoolmates. Is Toucinho a symbol for the African who, to maintain social position, serves Europeans by oppressing his brothers? A student of colonialism has remarked that many of the Europeans who went to Africa were weak men needing to assert their sense of self-value by dominating the African; failures in their own society, they could only gain self-respect by placing themselves in a superior position, a position of power in which they could freely insult or even kill those under their control. In his story Honwana indirectly supports such a view.

"Dina" is another story of humiliation and suffering caused by an insensitive and oppressive colonialism. Madala, an old man, works long gruelling hours under the heat of the sun in the corn fields. Physical and emotional pain are his constant companions. The corn fields of "Mulungo" (the white man in Ronga) are like the sea; they are apparently endless. The Clearing Gang, the Kraal Gang, and the Hoeing Gang of Africans gain little profit from working in these fields that the white man has taken for himself.

In another story, "Nhinguitimo," the whites, who control nearly all the land, take over the lands of Goana, particularly the rich soil of Virgula Oito that lies along the waters of the Incomati. Virgula Oito works the lands of the white man Rodrigues and only works his own fields when he is not working for the European. But the whites want all the land for themselves. Even though Virgula's ancestors are buried there, even though his entire family belongs to Goana, he must give up his land to Lodrica (mispronounciation of "Rodrigues") and other whites despite the fact that the latter own shops, tractors and large farms. Virgula rebels; he kills several people who try to capture him. At the end of the story Rodrigues and his friends take their guns and plan to shoot Virgula before something terrible happens in the village. They do not realize that something terrible has already happened, that the blacks have seen their lands stolen from them.

In "Dina" not only is the land the property of the whites but so also are the women. After Pitarossi died from the bite of a snake which had attacked him when he was working in the field, his wife would sleep with any "magaíca" (returning migrant laborer) who would buy her a drink. Her poverty and loneliness, caused primarily by the insensitivity of the Europeans, who fail to provide her with any help, results in her abasement. Equally sad is the plight of Maria, the daughter of Madala, the old man. While the old man is eating his "dina," the white overseer talks with Maria. He invites her to walk with him into the fields where they will plan an evening rendez-vous, but he cannot wait until evening. The overseer rapes Maria, after which he tosses her a coin. Poor Madala has witnessed the cruel defiling of his daughter. His humiliation is unbearable, but he is old and weak. The overseer, who refers to the workers as black swine, gives him some wine and when Madala swallows it in one gulp, the Kraal gang spits at his feet, for the old man has lost all dignity. He has added to his humiliation by accepting the insulting recompense offered by the overseer. The boss is a monster who breaks a bottle over the head of a youth who does not move quickly enough. He is like the administrator in "Nós Matámos o Cão-Tinhoso" a weak man compelled to inflict pain on others to prove his power.

Honwana does not tell us Madala's thoughts, but in "Papá, Cobra e Eu" we are permitted to enter the mind of a man who has had to endure humiliation and has remained silent. Ginho, the narrator, lives with his brothers and sisters and their parents outside the city. When it is discovered that a snake has been killing chickens and eating their eggs, it is determined that the snake must be killed. Ginho enters the chicken run, removes the blocks that had been stored there, and discovers the dark mamba, its black forked tongue quivering menacingly. Ginho and Nandito, his younger brother, who is unaware of the serpent's presence, sit down to chat. Nandito is frightened of snakes; he has heard that snakebite can kill a man unless the snake is burnt, dried and then eaten.

Ginho plays on his brother's fright, for he talks only about snakes. He must assert his superiority by intimidation. Totó, the family dog and o Lobo, the hunting dog of Senhor Castro, enter the chicken run. O Lobo barks frenetically upon spying the snake, who strikes the poor dog full on the chest. O Lobo runs home to die. When Senhor Castro hears from "his blacks" that his pointer came howling from the chicken run of Tchembene, Ginho's father, he immediately drives his car to Ginho's house. He demands compensation from Tchembene who, in his eyes, is reponsible for the death of his dog:

> O Tchemebne. . .Eu não estou para muitas conversas e só te digo isto: ou pagas uma idemnização ou faço queixa à Administração! Resolve! Era o melhor perdigueiro que jamais tive. . .[1]

> Tchembene. . . I'm not here for any backtalk, and I'm telling you: either you pay compensation or I'll make a formal complaint to the Administration! He was the best pointer I ever had. . .

Senhor Castro refuses to listen to Tchembene's explanation. Moreover, he arrogantly chastises him, claiming that a beating is what he deserves. When the white man departs, Ginho's father explains his pain:

> —Meu filho, tem de haver uma esperança! Quando um dia acaba e sabemos que amanhã sera tudo igualzinho, temos de ir arranjar forças para continuar a sorrir e continuar a dizer 'isso não tem importância!. . .Ainda hoje viste o senhor Castro a enxovalhar-me! Isso foi só um bocadinho da ração de hoje. . .Não, meu filho, mesmo que isto todo só O negue, Ele tem de existir!
>
>   O Papa parou de repente e sorriu num esforço. Depois acrescentou.
> —Mesmo um pobre tem de ter qualquer coisa. . .Mesmo que seja só uma esperança!. . Mesmo que ela seja falsa!. . .[2]

> —My son, one must have a hope! When the day is over and we know that the next day will be exactly the same, we need to find the strength to continue smiling and to continue saying "This isn't important!". . .Yet today you witnessed Senhor Castro humiliate me! This was only one small portion of today's ration. . .No my son, even if all this denies His existence, He must exist!

Papa suddenly stopped and forced himself to smile. Then he added, —Even a poor man has to have something...Even if it may be only hope!....Even if it may be false!...

Tchembene must fight continually for his manhood. He admits that, like his son, he has had to grow up repressing his hatred and his frustration; he has suffered much. And he is not even sure that his passivity is any safer or wiser than Ginho's overt hostility towards their oppressors. He tells his wife:

—Não é nada, mulher, mas o nosso filho acha que ninguem monta em cavalos diodas, e que nos famintos e mansos é onde lhes dá mais jeito, percebeste? Quando um cavalo endoidece dá-se-lhe um tiro e tudo acaba, mas aos cavalos mansos mata-se todos os dias. Todos os dias, ouviste? Todos, todos, todos enquanto eles se aguentarem de pé!...[3]

—It's nothing woman, but our son thinks that no one rides a difficult horse and that people prefer easy, frail ones. When a horse becomes wild, they shoot it and it's all finished, but meek horses are killed every day. Every day, do you hear? Day after day after day as long as they are able to stand!...

That Honwana chooses to speak of wild and docile animals is significant, for Mangy-Dog, who was not a threat to anyone, was killed as brutally as if he had been an aggressive dog. For the oppressed it does not seem that kindness and patience offer a path to a better future. Like Madala, Tchembene is afraid, but unlike the old man, he has a son who may find a way to a life of freedom and dignity. "Papá, Cobra e Eu" implies that perhaps violence is the only alternative left a people who receive only humiliation and degradation for their meekness.

The other three stories in *Nós Matámos o Cão-Tinhoso* are extremely short. In fact, it would be an exaggeration to call two of them short stories. "As Mãos dos Pretos" (The Hands of the Blacks), for instance, presents a series of myths explaining the light color of the palms of the black man. Of course the ludicrous interpretations provided by various white folk are so absurd as to evoke laughter, but behind such presentations lies racial prejudice. Dona Dores believes God made the palms lighter so black men wouldn't dirty the food they made for their masters. O Senhor Profesor believes that a few centuries ago black men walked around on all fours like wild animals; o Senhor Padre believes that they went about with their hands folded together, for they were silently praying; o Senhor Antunes, the Coca Cola man, claims that blacks were created in the kilns of heaven, but since the molds of clay were hung in chimneys, the smoke from the fire darkened their bodies; only their hands, with which they held on, were spared. Senhor Frias has an equally original interpretation: after God made people, he told them to bathe in a lake in heaven, but the blacks, who were made early in the morning when the water was very cold, only wet the palms of their hands and the soles of their feet. The narrator's mother offers the sanest answer to the question; the palms of the hands of blacks are light to show that what men do is nothing but the work of men, and that what men do is done by hands that are the same, for if people would stop to think, they would see that men "antes de serem qualquer outra coisa são homens" (before being anything else, are men). In this story Honwana again shows, with great subtlety, the psychology of racism.

"A Velha Mulher" (The Old Woman) is the tale of a loving mother who endures the suffering of her son who has been assaulted and humiliated in a bar by whites. She is warm, generous, unselfish; yet she is politically indifferent; she chooses not to understand, although she does realize that her son is a victim because he chooses to stand fast and be proud. She offers the only security he knows. Honwana is always sympathetic to old men and women who have had to smile at the white man while secretly they were suffering and knew pain; for these people endured, and made it possible for a later generation to change the direction of Society in Mozambique.

Honwana inherits a tradition of understated social protest in Mozambique. João Dias in his celebrated story "godido" and Orlando de Albuquerque in some of his stories depict in a gentle tone the plight of the African who is torn between his past and an unknown future in a world ripped apart by authoritarian and greedy Europeans. Ultimately, Honwana must be seen as a social writer, voicing the pain and sadness of the people of Mozambique. His simplicity of narrative is accompanied by a profound insight into the psychological dehumanization of both black and white living under a system that ultimately destroys the best instincts of all men. Since Honwana first wrote the stories in *Nós Matámos o Cão-Tinhoso,* the passive but tenacious Africans of Mozambique became less passive and under the leadership of Samora Machel fought and won the battle for independence. The lives of humiliation need continue no longer.

Footnotes

1. Luís Bernardo Honwana, "Papá, Cobra e Eu," in *Antologia do Conto Ultramarino,* ed. by Amândio César, (Lisbon, Editorial Verbo, 1972), p. 200.

2. *Ibid,* pp. 201-202.

3. *Ibid,* p. 202.

EIGHT POEMS BY BESSA VICTOR
(and translations by D. Burness)

A VELHA MULEMBA

Aquela velha mulemba...
Vieram homens armados
de catanas e machados,
duros de corpo e alma
(onde a bondade não medra),
mandados por alguém de coração de pedra,
—e assim, em nome da lei,
derrubaram e mataram
aquela velha mulemba,
velha rainha sem rei.

Não sofreram, não choraram;
só eu chorei!

Minha velha mulemba...
À sombra dela (eu era monandengue),
com outros meninos brincando,
eu ensaiei meus passos de massemba...
Tantas vezes ali deitei meu luando
e ali fiquei cochilanda.
'a sombra da mulemba

Só eu chorei de saudade,
quando a vi, hoje, caída,
morta. Foi como se fosse
a morte da minha vida!

Você, leitor, que me está lendo,
vai dizer-me assim, com espanto:
—Porque sofre você? Eu não entendo
o motivo do seu pranto.
Derrubaram cajueiro,
onde você comeu bom caju, tanto e tanto;
derrrubaram embondeiro,
onde você comeu muita múcua, no gozo;
derrubaram também tamarindeiro,
onde você comeu tamarindo gostoso...
Derrubaram essas árvores
que lhe deram sombra e fruto;
e você ficou na mesma como um bruto,
não sentiu então o dó

THAT OLD MULEMBA

That old mulemba . . .

Men armed with machetes
and axes came,
hardened in body and soul
(where goodness is not sown)
ordered by someone with a heart of stone,
—and thus, in the name of the law,
they demolished and killed
that old mulemba,
old queen without a king.

They did not suffer, they did not cry;
I alone cried;

My old mulemba . . .
Under its shade (I was a kid),
playing with other children,
I tried a step of the massemba[1] . . .
So many times I stretched out my mat
and there did sums
under the shade of the mulemba.

Alone I cried from nostalgic yearning,
when today I saw it fallen,
dead. It was as if
it were the death of my own life!

You, reader, who are reading me,
you are going to tell me with surprise:
Why do you suffer? I do not understand
The cause of your weeping.
They cut down a cashew-tree,
where you ate so many good cashew nuts;
they cut down a baobab,
where you savoured many mucuas;
they also cut down a tamarind-tree
where you ate the tasty tamarind.
They cut down those trees
that provided you shade and fruit;
and you remained like a beast,
you did not feel then the compassion

que tem da velha mulemba,
que so͏́ lhe deu sombra, so!—

Ninguém pode compreender
a dor da minha saudade,
isto que me faz sofrer!

Você, leitor, que me esta á ler,
queira notar esta verdade
que nâo me sai mais de lembrança:

—Uma vez, em criança,
puxei os bigodes do meu avô velho;
deu-me uma bofetada,
que minha cara negra ficou logo encarnada.
Pois, por muitos anos, eu andei puxando,
dia a dia, as barbas da velha mulemba,
nelas fiz balouço, fiquei balouçando;
e a velha mulemba não ficou zangada,
nunca me fez nada,
nem um so͏́ açoite, nem um so͏́ lamento,
senão a carícia das susa longas barbas
no meu rosto, no meu corpo, quando o vento
as beijava e fazia estremecer . . .—

Minha velha mulemba . . .
Ah, so͏́ eu sei o que me faz sofrer!

that you now have for the old mulemba,
that gave you nothing but shade!

No one can understand
the grief of my longing,
which causes me to suffer!

You, reader who are reading me,
please note this truth
which I can never forget.

—Once as a boy
I tugged at the mustaches of my old grandfather;
he gave a slap,
so that my black face turned red.
So, for many years, day after day,
I used to pull the branches of the old mulemba,
out of them I made a swing to play;
and the old mulemba never became angry,
never did anything to me,
not a single slap, not a single lament,
other than the strokings of the long beard
on my face, on my body, when the wind
was kissing and shaking it . . .

My old mulemba . . .
Ah! I alone know what makes me suffer!

---

[1] Traditional Angolan dance from which, in terminology and choreography, the Brazilian Samba is derived.

O MENINO E O BALAO

Menino negro, cujo balão voa
no céu afogueado da sanzala
mais alto do que o sonho que te inspira,
aos ventos vou lançar o balão da mentira
onde escondo nas ruas de Lisboa
a saudade angolana que me embala.

THE BLACK CHILD AND THE KITE

Black child, whose kite[1] flies
in the inflamed sky of the sanzala[2]—
higher than the dreams that inspire you,
to the winds I will throw my kite of lies
where in the streets of Lisbon
I conceal my sad longing for Angolan skies
      which lulls me to sleep.

---

[1] "Balão," the Portugese word for "kite," is also a Brazilian slang word for "lie."
[2] Poor section in the suburbs of an Angolan city.

SOU OUTRA VEZ MENINO

Na orquestra do "cabaret"
deste prédio grandioso,
está sepultado o gemido
de antiga cubata morta.

O piano assenta sobre
os escombros da marimba.
O vinho do Porto suga
restos de extinto quimbombo.

Este homem, que sou agora,
oculta aquele menino,
que em mim houve, o monandengue
a quem a festa do baile
era sonho proibido . . .

Não sei que mistério fundo,
súbito, me transfigura.
Eu sou outra vez menino:
visto de nova o meu bibe,
mas já sem medo da noite,
nem dos homens nem de nada,
entro nas salas de dança,
ando pelas ruas fora,
enchendo a alma do povo,
com o som do meu berimbau
e a música dos meus muimbos,
até que a manhã me acorde.

I AM AGAIN A CHILD

In the orchestra of the "cabaret"
of this grandiose building
is buried the groan
of an old dead African hut.

The piano rests on
the ruins of the marimba.
The wine from Porto sucks
remnants of extinct quimbombo.

The man, that I am now,
hides that child,
which I had within me, the monandengue
to whom the formal dance
was a forbidden dream . . .

I do not know what profound mystery,
suddenly, transfigures me.
I am again a child:
Seen again my child's smock,
but now without fear of the night,
neither of men nor of anything,
I enter the dance halls,
I walk crazily the streets,
filling the soul of the people,
with the sound of my jew's harp
and the music of my muimbos,
until the morning awakens me.

APONTAMENTO NA QUITANDA DO MUCEQUE

Na quitanda do muceque
de S. Paulo de Luanda,
o menino negro chupa sorvete,
o menino branco come quitaba,
ambos sorrindo, ambos cantando
a *Maria Candimba, o Abril em Portugal.*

E a minha alma de poeta
—alma mestiça, luso-tropical—
descobre acenos de Africa
no gesto do menino branco
e visões da Europa
no olhar do menino negro.

NOTE ON A SHOP IN THE MUCEQUE

In the shop in the muceque
of S. Paulo de Luanda,
a black child is sucking sherbet,
a white child is eating quitaba,
both smiling, both singing
the first *Maria Candimba,* the second *April in Portugal.*

And my poet's soul
—a hybrid soul, luso-tropical—
discerns signs of Africa
in the gesture of the white child
and visions of Europe
in the look of the black child.

O NEGRO VAGABUNDO

*Eu vou nesta viagem pelo mundo.
E há vozes que perguntam:*—Quem é ele?
Há uma voz que responde:—É um vagabundo;
uma força secreta, estranha, o impele.

*Vou por caminhos de variados rumos.
E ha vozes que perguntam:*—Donde vem ele? Donde? . . .
—Vem de terras e mares ignorados,
há uma voz que responde.

*Então canto os meus versos de poeta.
E mil vozes perguntam:*—Que pretendes?
Que bens compras ou vendes?
Qual é a tue meta?
Donde vem o teu sonho e para onde vai,
nesta longa viagem?

Eis a Voz do Universo:—Em silêncio, escutai,
mercenários da alma, calai vossa linguagem
de ganância e vaidade.
O poeta negro traz ao mundo uma mensagem
de amor e fraternidade.

THE VAGABOND NEGRO

I go on this journey through the world.
And voices ask:—Who is he?
A voice responds: He is a vagabond;
a secret and strange force impels him.

My trip takes me on various paths.
And voices ask: Where does he come from?
A voice responds:
He comes from lands and seas unknown.

And so, a poet, I sing my verses.
And a thousand voices ask: What do you want?
What goods are you buying or selling?
What is your goal?
What do your dreams come from? Where do they take you—
on this long journey?

Here is the Voice of the Universe: Listen, quietly,
mercenaries of the soul; silence your tongues
of cupidity and vanity.
The black poet brings to the world a message
of love and brotherhood.

O MEU CORAÇÃO BATUCA

Meu coração batuca ao ritmo e som
das marimbas, quingufos e quissanges.
(O batuque nasceu comigo, o ser me invade,
e sinto-o no meu sangue,
desde essa hora,
no movimento inicial da minha liberdade,
no canto com que sadei a terra, a humanidade.)
Dentro da minha alma canta e chora
todo o grito dos muimbos africanos.
O fogo da queimada no capim
e´a febre que me avassala,
quando o teu corpo e o meu requebram na sanzala,
onde, uma noite, ainda monandengues,
fizemos bailar o amor.

Neste mesmo instante, na Europa longe,
nos salões requintados de Londres,
de Roma, de Paris, de Madrid ou Lisboa,
grupos de jovens, dançando e cantando,
disfarçados, estão macaqueando
a nossa batucada que no mundo ressoa.
Eles cantam e dançam
—movimento e alarido,
vozes e pernas . . .
Mas nós temos na carne e na alma,
desde o primeiro gesto e o primeiro vagido,
o ritmo e o som deste batuque,
a voz de África eterna.

MY HEART BEATS

My heart beats to the rhythm and sound
of marimbas, quingufos[1] and quissanges.[2]
(The batuque was born with me, its essence invades me,
and I have felt it in my blood,
from that hour,
in the initial movement of my liberty,
in the chant with which I greet earth, humanity.)
Within my soul the echo
of African muimbos[3] sings and cries.
The fire of the burning in the grass
is the fever which overwhelms me,
when your body and mine sway in the sanzala,[4]
where, one night, still monandengues[5]
we made the love dance.

At this same moment, in far away Europe,
in the refined parlors of Paris,
Rome, London, Madrid or Lisbon,,
groups of young people, dancing and singing,
masquerading, are mimicking
our African rhythm which resounds throughout the world.
They are singing and dancing
—movement and clamor,
voices and legs. . .
But we have in our body and in our spirit,
from the first gesture and the first baby's cry,
the rhythm and sound of this batuque[6]
the voice of Africa eternal.

---

[1] A kind of drum.
[2] Musical instrument played by fingering.
[3] Songs.
[4] Poor section in the suburbs of an Angolan city.
[5] Children.
[6] Any of several African dances.

ULTIMO CANTO DO MARACACHÃO

Canta, canta, meu balacaxongo!

Que é feito das canções que me ensinaste,
os muimbos com que embalaste,
em manhãs de vendaval, em noites de cazumbis,
em momentos de sonho, em instantes febris,
o neto dos mues avós?

Hoje tudo mudou para nós.
O secular cajueiro,
onde ambos assobiámos assombrando
tudo e todos com nosso alegre canto,
não existe: não mais dará fruto nem sombra.
(O pranto dos meus olhos é de espanto!)
O sumo do caju que outrora debicaste
põe notas lacrimosas na tua voz.

Não és o mesmo balacaxongo
de antigamente.
(Que voz é essa? Ignoro essa cantiga
que me descomanda.)
Viajei pela Europa, pelo mundo,
vi outra gente, e já não sou o camundongo
da antiga Luanda.

Não reconheço em ti o cantador
que me encantava o coração.
Não descobres em mim (realidade ou quimera?),
homem disfarçado que sou,
o monandengue autêntico que eu era.

Canta para mim, mais uma vez, balacaxongo.
Ah, não, não cantes mais, maracachão!

LAST SONG OF THE MARACACHÃO[1]

Sing, sing, my balacaxongo![2]

What has become of the songs you taught me,
the muimbos[3] with which you lulled to sleep,
the grandson of my ancestors,
in mornings when the wind roared, in nights of cazumbis,[4]
during the short-lived dreams or feverish moments?

Today everything has changed for us.
The secular cashew-tree,
where we both used to whistle startling
the world with our happy trill,
does not exist: no longer will it provide fruit or shade.
(A feeling of astonishment makes me weep!)
The juice from the cashew-nut you once picked
produces lachrymose notes in your song.

You are no longer the balacaxongo
of times past.
(What voice is that? I ignore that song
which no longer directs me.)
I have traveled through Europe, through the world,
I have seen other people, and no longer am I the camundongo[5]
of old Luanda.

I do not recognize in you the singer
that used to enchant my heart.
You do not find in me (reality or chimera?),
counterfeit man that I am,
the authentic monandengue that I was.

Sing for me, one more time, balacaxongo
Ah, no, sing no more, maracachão!

---

[1] A beautiful bird (Portuguese rendering of Quimbundo 'mbalakaxongo') with a melodious song.
[2] Another name for 'maracachão'.
[3] Songs.
[4] Spirit of another world.
[5] Nickname meaning 'little mouse' that is usually used to refer to a boy from Luanda.

NATAL

(poema em prosa)

Há anos, na noite de Natal, numa cubata do mato angolense, uma família de tribo indígena, em cujos corações já soara a mensagem divina através da palavra portuguesa, celebrava, na sua ingenuidade pitoresca, o nascimento do Filho de Deus, à maneira da civilização cristã.

Havia uma nota originalíssima no figurativo quadro clássico. Ao canto da cubata estava construido um pequeno presépio feito de adobe, com capim e folhas de palmeira, com os reis magos e pastorinhos e, deitado em esteira de mabu, o monandengue Jesus, boneco feito de pau, pintado de preto.

Eis o milagre do amor no Natal de Cristo.

Há vinte séculos Jesus Cristo nasceu, numa manjedoura, em Belém de Judeia. Mas todos os anos através dos tempos, neste dia, Ele nasce nos palácios sumptuosos e choupanas da Ásia, nas vivendas ricas e casinhotas da Europa, nos arranha-céus colossais e bairros pobres das Américas, nas cidades e vilas da África, sob a música dos sinos e das harpas, e já nas sanzalas típicas da África Negra, ao som dos quissanges e marimbas.

Na sua materialidade exótica, aquele quadro da cubata revelava a verdade eterna do espírito, não ofendida nem falseada: Jesus nasce no coração de cada ser humano, em todos os povos e raças, porque Ele é, milagrosamente, e Deus-Menino de toda a gente.

CHRISTMAS
(A Prose Poem)

Years ago, on Christmas night in a hut of Angolan brushwood, a family of an indigenous tribe in whose hearts had already sounded the divine message through Portuguese word, were celebrating in their picturesque ingenuousness the birth of the Son of God, in the way of Christian civilization.

It made a most original comment on a symbolic classical painting. At the corner of the hut was constructed a small creche made of adobe, with grass and palm leaves, with the magical kings and little shepherds, and placed on a mat of mabu, the monandengue Jesus, a doll made of wood, painted in black.

Behold the miracle of love on the birth of Christ.

Twenty centuries ago Jesus Christ was born in a manger in Bethlehem of Judea. But every year throughout the ages on this day, He is born in sumptuous palaces and huts of Asis, in the rich lodgings and shanties of Europe, in the colossal skyscrapers and poor neighborhoods of the Americas, in the cities and small towns of Africa, to the music of bells and harps, and presently in the typical sanzalas of black Africa, to the sound of quissanges and marimbas.

In its exotic materiality, that picture of the hut was revealing the eternal truth of the spirit, neither offended nor falsified: Jesus is born in the heart of every human being, in all people and races, because He is, miraculously, the God-Child of all people.

AFTERWORD

This project of Donald Burness incorporates the study of authors who punctuate three areas of African literature of Portuguese expression: Cape Verde, Angola and Mozambique. Given the fact that there has not appeared as of the present date an author of renown in Guiné-Bissau,[1] the only omission will be S. Tome e Príncipe which possess an interesting group of poets: Caetano da Costa Alegre, Marcelo Veiga, Francisco José Tenreiro, Alda do Espírito Santo, Tomás Medeiros, Maria Manuela Margarido.

But the intention of Donald Burness is to study specific cases, without covering all Lusophone areas. To demand something else would be to propose another book, another project. Besides discussing and applauding his proposal, we are also interested in it because it seems to us opportune in a work of this nature to raise some questions, some basic and others of a general nature, which determine the physiognomy of African Literature of Portuguese expression, and, moreover, to draw the attention of persons interested in this literature which is the product of specific historical and cultural phenomena.[2] Besides, Donald Burness refers to some of these subjects appropriately in his introduction, which is an excellent augury.

An elementary affirmation: African Literature in the Portuguese language is born of a colonial *corpus,* and emerges later from a complex fabric through the contact of cultures. It reflects, essentially, a forced situation in five autonomous areas not even geographically neighboring one another. The first point of discussion concerns whether the effects of colonization were identical in all these areas. The answer is that at least in the case of Cape Verde, it is individual. Very early, thanks to a very wide and profound ethnic and cultural miscegenation, the Cape-Verdean mulatto (who comprises over two thirds of the population) acquired a singular personality and developed his own culture, functioning in diverse sectors and at various levels—in education, in administration, in the bureaucracy—areas generally controlled by Europeans. This is equivalent to saying that the contact of cultures occurred under circumstances that went beyond mere cultural juxtaposition or dominance, and that from the initial cultural incompatibility and instability there evolved a syncretism, a harmonization of the Cape-Verdean personality.

Today, inexorably, Cape Verde has its historic destiny tied to that of Africa and the Republic of Guiné-Bissau. Geographic, economic, and political factors determined it. Yet it would be excessive to consider the Archipelago of Cape Verde from a cultural point of view as an African totality, as has already been polemically affirmed. We defend the specificity of Cape-Verdean culture with the knowledge that we are not dealing with a unique case on the African continent. Such an African totality certainly exists in Africa south of the Sahara. This is not the case in Islamic North Africa. Or if we turn our attention to the Carribbean the case of Cuba is similar to that of Cape Verde.

We are in fact concerned with a new culture, a Cape-Verdean culture, marked by specific elements in various planes of its daily life: in food, in music, in popular poetry, in dance, in oral literature, in methods of production, in the economy, in multiple and various features or patterns of culture such as marriage, celebrations, domestic life and the monogamic system. And moreover this is true even on a linguistic plane since the Crioulo dialect has been so profoundly implanted that it is nothing less than the Cape-Verdean language. This makes the Cape-Verdean bilingual orally and literarily. As writers of the *mornas* and the *coladeiras,* always in Crioulo, Eugénio Tavares, José Bernardo Alfama, Pedro Cardoso stand out as pioneers and their successors in recent decades include Sergio Frusoni, Ovídio Martins, Kaoberdiano Dambará and others. The Cape-Verdean language is reconstructed from 15th century Portuguese and if at times there were syntactic borrowings from autochthonous African languages, nevertheless according to the knowledgeable voice of Baltasar Lopes da Silva, at least 97% of all words are of Portuguese origin (see *O dialecto crioulo de Cabo Verde,* 1957).

We agree in principle with those who believe that the Archipelago of Cape Verde, now free of colonial oppression, has acquired the precise conditions so that the African roots of its culture, which for centuries were denigated, can once again be the basis of a modern Cape-Verdean culture. This can be accepted; it is even legitimate to desire it, but only the future will decide the true cultural destiny of the Cape-Verdean man once his political destiny is defined according to the precepts of Amilcar Cabral. But for now we cannot ignore the situation as it is.

In this context the cultural area which is closest to Cape Verde is that of the Archipelago of S. Tomé e Príncipe, given that until the end of the 19th century it suffered a joint historical-cultural evolution (see Francisco José Tenreiro: *Cabo Verde e São Tomé e Príncipe, Esquema de uma Evolução Conjunta,* 1950). Here too a crioulo dialect was created, living, co-existing with the Portuguese language, without having in the meantime enjoyed the importance which the Crioulo dialect acquired in Cape-Verdean society. And other patterns of European culture associated themselves with or melted into the African culture. The case of *Tchiloli* is one of the best examples. It deals with a long tradition of popular 15th century theatre based, presumably, on a play by the Portuguese playwright Baltasar Dias, a native of the island of Madeira, a play which is appreciated and enthusiastically received by people of S. Tomé e Príncipe. This a curious and impressive adaptation of an alien culture, intelligently reelaborated and spontaneously recreated.

In Angola and Mozambique and even in Guiné-Bissau the path of evolution was vastly different. A very limited European penetration, along the littoral, expanded from the end of the 19th century (Berlin Conference, 1885, English Ultimatum to Portugal, 1890), but even then cultural contacts were primarily limited to the principal urban centers. There a substantial mulatto population developed (more in Angolan cities than those of Mozambique) inhibiting in some of them, like Luanda, the formation of subcultures. And this resulted in a coming together of men and races who shared a common oppression and repression. However, blatant manifestations of racism emerged through economic and political exploitation by the colonial regime.

But because it was in cities that industry and commerce developed, schools were created, cultural centers were organized, journalism flourished, and there also an atmosphere was created that propitiated the appearance of intellectuals and writers. The present literature of Mozambique and Angola is a literature marked by the growth of a mulatto population. We shall examine this more closely later.

If in Cape Verde a unique literature in harmony with the nature of its social structures was created encompassing the Cape-Verdean totality, it is natural to ask if in the other African countries something similar occurred. In a way, yes; in a way, no. In Angola and Mozambique, apart from the urban centers and limitrophe areas, the land was maintained by traditional societies, vast tribal zones; and in intermediate areas, were found those who suffered the partial effects of detribalization. In these countries, genuine African traditions were not uprooted throughout most of the territory: methods of production, social hierarchies, an oral literature, mythology, a philosophy of life, a history—these had been shared by African people for many centuries.

The other component to be examined is that which took place in the detribalized areas, especially in the urban centers, where an economy of subsistance was replaced by an economy of trade at the market place. And the Portuguese language became dominant over, especially in social relations, (even though not always in domestic relations) the autochthonous languages. The literatures of Angola and Mozambique (the case of S. Tomé e Príncipe always considered as an intermediate case) are the consequence of this coming together: countries of a certain cultural fragmentation and writers whose experience, if not exclusively, is primarily urban. There has been a relatively small influence exerted by those societies sometimes called "primitive" or traditional.

It is from experience in those areas punctuated by the presence of two cultures that the poets and narrators developed their works. Moreover, it is evident that this literature manifests a profound national and nationalistic stamp. After the forties, the modern Angolan and Mozambican (and S. Tomesian) authors, especially the poets, thanks to clandestine political involvement, acquired a national consciousness and undertook the task of expressing not only their own personal experiences in a racially mixed culture, but also the general drama of Angolans or Mozambicans, and a solidarity with all Africans. The echo of this drama was reaching them through Countee Cullen, Langston Hughes, Guillén, Jacques Roumain, and others.

> Tua presença, minha Mãe-drama vivo de una Raça
> drama de carne e sangue
> Que a vida escreveu com a pena de séculos,
> Pela tua voz
>   Vozes vindas dos canaviais dos arrozais dos
>   cafezais dos seringais dos algodais. . . !
> Vozes das plantações da Virgínia
> dos Campos das Carolinas
> Alabama
>   Cuba
>   Brasil. . .
> Vozes dos engenhos dos banguês das tongas dos eitos
>   das pampas das usinas!
> Vozes de Harlem Hill District South
>   vozes das sanzalas
> Vozes gemendo *Blues*, subindo o *Mississippi*, ecoando
> Vozes chorando na voz de Carrothers:
>   *Lord God, what have we done*
> —Vozes de toda America, Vozes de toda África.
> Vozes de todas as vozes, na voz altiva de Langston
>   Na bela vox de Guillén. . . [3]

Thus it would be wrong to consider these literatures as amputated. On the contrary, even admitting a certain scantiness or absence in the literary transfiguration of certain structures, they share an expression of a common suffering or an anti-colonial consciousness. And we say anti-colonial consciousness because this is the dominant theme which justifies and clarifies the literary production of these last decades, particularly in poetry. Its message which is by no means hermetic does permit a vast world of meanings and is punctuated by the expression of conflicts, ruptures, alienations, anxieties and tensions. Nothing is innocent in this writing. And one of its more notable achievements is that it foreshadows the struggle for liberation. We need only look over some titles of poems that present us with a prophetic semantics: "Certeza" ("Certainty"—Agostinho Neto), "Poema da Amanhã" ("Poem of Tomorrow"—António Nunes), "Quando a Vida Nascer" ("When Life is Born"—Mário Fonseca), "Deixa Passar o meu Povo" ("Let my people go"—Noémia de Sousa), "Aviso" ("Warning"—Ovídio Martins), "O novo canto da Mãe" ("The mother's new song"—Tomás Medeiros).

But beyond these titles charged with unsuspected metaphorical assertion there is the conviction of a poetry that does not leave room for ambiguities. Or, if it allows them, they are the fruit of circumlocutory expression, metaphorical or metonymical, made necessary by the loss of freedom of expression as well as police repression (a context that was practically unknown to authors in English or French). But the "resolution of ambiguity" is within our reach. One example only, for economy's sake, and a rather simple one. "Vem!/ Dá-me a tua mão!/ Entra no terreiro/ e dança com Mãe-Bia/ este batuque verde!/"—Gabriel Mariano, (Come!/Give me your hand!/ Enter into the square/ and dance with Mama Bia/ this green batuque). The call for the creation of a collective consciousness and participation in the common struggle, a breath of hope (batuque verde) in a free future, ends up being quite clear.

It is easy at first reading to recognize whether we are dealing with a Cape-Verdean text rather than one from Angola or Mozambique. The lexical ground and in certain cases the semantic are not coincidental. In addition to linguistic acquisitions common to these cultural areas, in Cape Verde the Portuguese language, reflecting a unique social process, as we have seen, is punctuated by frequent diminutives and frequent borrowings from the Crioulo dialect. Consequently, the prose or poetry of Cape Verde frequently resembles Brazilian writings. It is, however, far more difficult for us to distinguish an Angolan from a Mozambican text. This obviously may not be the case for those closely familiar with the social reality of these countries, or for those who may be master of the "situação do discurso" of these literatures. Knowledge of linguistic elements and certain cultural values in particular geographical areas where there was miscegenation, help our decodification. But even if we use such extra-literary evidence the deciphering does not come quickly. It may seem relatively easy in terms of external structure, but it is far more difficult in terms of profound understanding. Despite the existence of different ethnic societies, Angola and Mozambique do share a common culture and history. Only through an evolution that history will determine can each of the two indigenous language literatures find its own special character.

In spite of everything which we have affirmed, we think that Angolan and Mozambican literature present distinctions, a complex fact whose analysis demands unceasing study. This is not perhaps the moment to undertake it, but having gone this far we should add two further points. If in the literature of Angola and Mozambique the protagonists are identified by the color of their skin (white, black, mulatto) and racial tensions often provide the substance to develop the narrative or poetry, Cape-Verdean literature by its very nature ignores such references. Another distinctive note is that which comes from *négritude*. While this helps to enrich those other literatures, in Cape Verde it gives way to "Cabo-verdianidade," the expression of a society whose consciousness of color has been diluted and whose cultural roots (one must have courage to say this) have lost their African memory.

Donald Burness calls attention to the uncommon circumstance of white Africans participating in the construction of this literature. And he even juxtaposes poets like Agostinho Neto (black), President of the People's Republic of Angola, and António Jacinto (white), present Minister of Education in the Angolan government. In fact the presence of white writers in the literature (and in the political and administrative life as well) of Angola and Mozambique is pronounced; some in fact were even pioneers. We are reminded for example of one Fonseca de Amaral (Mozambique) or the above mentioned António Jacinto, also a Luandino Vieira and more recently a David Mestre (Angola). Some are authors who were born there, but the last two went to Africa from Portugal at so tender an age that they learned to speak there and became Africans. There are cases, moreover, like Ruy de Carvalho, who even though he went at the age of twelve to Angola, made up his mind at the age of twenty! "Aqui me dei,/ Aqui me fiz,/ desfiz, refiz amores." (Here I got along,/ here I made myself,/ unmade, remade loves.) But a broadening of this phenomena is still another thing—the tendency on the part of Portuguese authors who, already grown men, traveled to Africa and became integrated in their new society. An example of this can be seen in the following lines of Candido da Velha:

> Mercer a tatuagem:
> beber nos rios do seu Povo,
> habitar nas cubatas de barro e de capim,

guardar suas mulheres de lua e noite
e os filhos do amor no coração.

Ter África no sangue
e compreender a voz dos quimbos
sénti-la como reza em noites de kazumbi,
noites de óbito e batuque nas sanzalas.

But the most extraordinary case is that of João Grabato Dias, (i.e. António Quadros) who disembarked in Maputo, capital of Mozambique, a little over ten years ago, and already at that time was known as a poet and painter in Portugal. After having published four books of poetry in Mozambique (and to speak the truth, only one of them with reference to Mozambique, and that merely to the city of Maputo), Grabato Dias, then Assistant Professor at the Faculty of Letters of that city, turned over to FRELIMO in the period of independence, the effects of a guerilla fighter killed in combat, Mutimati Barnabé João. Among the effects was a manuscript of the poem: *Eu e o Povo* (I and the People). The cultural services of FRELIMO edited the book and on the jacket is written: "Mutimati Barnabé João is an individual voice which incorporates the collective voice. *Eu e o Povo* is now the property of Mozambique; the people of Mozambique wrote it." Months later it became known that Mutimati Barnabé João was in fact Grabato Dias. And even then, in Mozambique and in Portugal, no one, not even the critics, doubted that this magnificent work was written by a Mozambican.

The fascist colonial Portuguese government after the Second World War demagogically defended the theses of multiraciality and multi-continentality, with the object of avoiding international attack. The idea of multiraciality was not, however, supported by the important writers. These had long ago chosen to defend the fundamental rights of the colonized and oppressed people. The official thesis was being defended by servant writers who defended the Portuguese presence in Africa, in the end staining and not defending a genuine African culture. To add to this support a few idealogues came forth who contemplated a putative Portuguese literature in Africa—or some others flowering in the luso-tropicality of Gilberto Freyre. The multiraciality currently defended by the MPLA or FRELIMO or PAIGC is of another fabric. And it reveals itself in the capacity for creative absorption in sundry domains: political, social, administrative and intellectual.

This white contribution must be one of the particulars that distinguishes African literature of Portuguese expression from the literature of the francophone or anglophone areas.

In this context one asks what is the place and destiny of this literature written until now (except for Cape Verde and sporadic cases in S. Tomé e Príncipe) exclusively in the Portuguese language?

In truth while one notes the existence of literatures in African languages like Ibo, Yoruba, Swahili, Xhosa, Zulu, Sotho, and others in Angola or Mozambique there is no written literature in Ronga, Quimbundo, Umbundo, for example, or in any other language which is not Portuguese.

The official Portuguese policy impeded the teaching of African languages in schools. During the fifty years of fascism, which was the period during which historical conditions could have favored such instructions, everything was done so that this would not happen. Adequate structures for such a project died at that time. Today, to build a solid base for instituting the teaching of African languages, those responsible for the destiny of the culture must realize that this institutionalization will take time. The governments are engaged at present in programs of literacy in the Portuguese language so that citizens may be able to participate more rapidly in the conscious process of national transformation and development. The resources will obviously not be such as to permit a parallel creation of structures for the teaching of national languages. But this is a question that goes beyond us and upon which we lack certain facts for a definitive judgment. Be it as it may, we believe we are not straying far from the truth in claiming that a favorable situation exists for African literature in the Portuguese language, no longer the standard Portuguese language but a language marked by ruptures and restructuring: a Mozambican language, an Angolan language, a Cape-Verdean language.

In his study Donald Burness examines four Angolan writers: Agostinho Neto, José Luandino Vieira, Mário António, Geraldo Bessa Victor; a Cape-Verdean, Baltasar Lopes; and one Mozambican, Luís Bernardo Honwana.

It is not unusual for an American university professor to be preoccupied with the study of African literature of Portuguese expression. We have several examples: the case of Gerald Moser, prestigious Lusophile to whom we are indebted for the valuable work which dates from his *Essays in Portuguese-African Literature* (1969), a work dedicated to Castro Soromenho, to his *Tentative Portuguese-African Bibliography: Portuguese Literature in Africa and African Literature in the Portuguese Language*[4] (1970); Richard A. Preto-Rodas with his meritorious *Negritude as a Theme in the Poetry of the Portuguese-Speaking World* (1970); Donald E. Herdeck who in his most important *African Authors* dedicated a reasonable number of notes to African writers of Portuguese expression; O.R. Dathorne, author of *Black Mind: A History of African Literature* (1974) with a section on African Literature of Portuguese expression. Mr. Dathorne also co-authored with another devoted specialist in African Literature of Anglophone and Francophone expression, Willfried Feuser, an anthology, *Africa in Prose*, in which he integrates Portuguese language authors; or Norman Araujo, a descendant of Cape-Verdeans, with his valuable *Study of Afro-Portuguese Literature* (1975); and, more recently, Russell G. Hamilton, author of the first global history of African Literature of Portuguese expression, a pioneering and definitive work in light of its structures and analytic consciousness, *Voices from an Empire/A History of Afro-Portuguese Literature* (1975). These and other works, including short essays (some of which we admit we do not know), like those of Eduardo Mayone Dias, are a genuine testimony to the interest which little by little, has been shown in the area of African Literature of Portuguese expression by university professors in the U.S.A. Donald Burness is not therefore the first from this continent to discover this ground, so little known and insufficiently studied, both abroad or in Portugal, or even in the new Portuguese African countries themselves, since only now have conditions been created for an in-depth propagation and study.

But the position of Donald Burness is a privileged one. His scholarly writing in the field of African literature in French, English and Portuguese have earned him the respect of many Africanists. His major contributions include articles and translations published in such journals as *Ba Shiru, Studies in Black Literature, Présence Africane* and *Okike* and especially his book *Shaka, King of the Zulus, in African Literature.* He also teaches African Literature of English and French expression at Franklin Pierce College.

This is very important because his bipolar experience gives him, uncontestably, a specific competence permitting him to understand and to point out unique characteristics of Portuguese African Literature. Such a capacity cannot be underestimated. Moreover, Donald Burness possesses along with his talent, an enthusiasm, a thirst for knowledge, and a desire to seek a shared communion.

Manuel Ferreira
University of Lisbon
1976

Footnotes

1. Note the narratives of the Cape-Verdean Fausto Duarte, who for many years lived in Guiné-Bissau; his work was somewhat influenced by the colonial epoch.

2. See Manuel Ferreira, *No Reino de Caliban: Antologia Panorâmica de Poesia Africana de Expressão Portuguesa.* 2nd Volume., Lisbon, Seara Nova, 1976.

3. Excerpt from the poem of Viriato da Cruz (Angolan, died in Pequim in 1973 and one of the founders of the MPLA): "Mamã Negra" (Canto de Esperança—A memória do poeta haitiano Jacques Roumain in *Poemas*, 1961). The poem, however, must have been written in the early years of the fifties.

4. Due for publication in 1978 (first semester) the *Bibliografia da Literatura Africana de Expressão Portuguesa* by Gerald Moser and Manuel Ferreira.

Selected Bibliography*

Vieira, Luandino
A Cidade e a Infância. Colecção Autores Ultramarinos, 2, Lisbon, Casa dos Estudantes do Império, 1960. (Short Stories)
Duas Historias de Pequenos Burgueses. Colecção Imbondeiro, 23, Sá da Bandeira, Imbondeiro, 1961. (Short Stories)
Vidas Novas. Vila da Maia, Afrontamento, 1975. (Short Stories)
"O Fato Completo de Lucas Matesso". (Story in *Vidas Novas* in *Novembre*, No. 4, l965 in Algeria. Also in French translation with "La Vraie Vie de Domingos Xavier," Paris, Présence Africaine, 1971.)
A Vida Verdadeira de Domingos Xavier. Lisbon, Edições 70, 1974. (Novel)
  French translation: Paris, Presénce Africaine, 1971.
  German translation: Berlin, Volk und Welt, 1974.
  Russian translation: Moscow, Inostrannaya Literatura, 1973.
  Swedish translation: In preparation.
Made into a film entitled *Sambizanga,* by Sarah Maldoror, 1972.
Luuanda. Luanda, ABC, 1963. (Short Stories)
  2nd edition, Belo Horizonte (Brazil), Eros, 1965.
  3rd edition, Lisbon, Edições 70, 1972.
Nós, os do Makulusu. Colecção Vozes do Mundo, Lisbon, Sá da Costa, 1974. (Novel)
No Antigamente na Vida. Lisbon, Edições 70,1974. (Short Stories)
Velhas Estorias. Lisbon, Plátano Editora, SARL, 1974. (Short Stories)
"Primeira Canção do Mar." Colecção Imbondeiro, 14, Sá da Bandeira, 1961. (Short Story)
"Os Muídos do Capitão Bento Albano." In *Novos Contos d' Africa,* Sá da Bandeira, 1962. (Short Story)

---

* All initial biographical entries are as complete as possible. Repeated entries list titles only.

Vieira, Luandino — Individual Poems Appear In:

Resistência Africana, ed. Serafim Ferreira, Colecção Universidade do Povo, 2. Lisbon, Diabril Editora, S.A.R.L., 1975.

No Reino de Caliban, Vol. II, ed. Manuel Ferreira, Lisbon, Seara Nova, 1976.

Poetas Angolanos, ed. Carlos Eduardo, Lisbon, Casa dos Estudantes do Império, 1959.

New Sum of Poetry from the Negro World, Paris, Présence Africaine, No. 57, 1966.

Présence Africaine, No. 47, First Trimester, 1966.

Vieira, Luandino — Critical Studies

Andrade, Mario de, "Noveau Langage dans L'Imaginaire Angolais", Preface to *La Vraie Vie de Domingos Xavier et Le Complet de Mateus,* Paris, Présence Africaine, 1971, pp. 7-18.

Garcia, José Martins, "Luandino Vieira: o anti-apartheid," *Colóquio,* No. 22, 1975.

Jacinto, Tomás, "The Art of Luandino Vieira," *Ba Shiru,* Vol. 5, No. 1, Fall, 1973, pp. 49-58.

Lemos, Virgílio de, Review of *Luuanda, Présence Africaine,* No. 58, Second Trimester, 1966.

Rassner, Ronald. "Colonialism and the Fiction of Luandino Vieira," a paper presented at Conference on Interdisciplinary Perspectives on Colonial and Neo-Colonial Africa," Northern Illinois University, Dekalb, Illinois, June 24-25, 1975.

Neto, Agostinho

Poemas. Colecção Autores Ultramarinos, 8, Lisbon, Casa dos Estudantes do Império, 1961. (Poetry)

Sagrada Esperança. Colecção, Vozes do Mundo, Lisbon, Sá da Costa, 1974. (Poetry)

   Italian translation: *Con Occhi Asciutti,* Milan, II Saggiatore, 1963.
   Serbo-Croation translation: *Ociju bez Suza,* Belgrad, Kultura, 1968.
   English translation: *Sacred Hope,* translated by Marga Holness, Dar es Salaam, Tanzania Publishing House, 1974.

"Nausea," In *Mensagem,* Luanda, and *Contistas Angolanos,* ed. by Fernando Mourão, Lisbon, Casa dos Estudantes do Império, 1960. (Short Story)

Neto, Agostinho — Individual Poems Appear In:

Resistência Africana.

No Reino de Caliban, Vol. II.

Antologia de Poesia Negra de Expressão Portuguesa, ed. by Mário de Andrade, Paris, P.J. Oswald, 1958.

Modern Poetry from Africa, ed. Gerald Moore and Ulli Beier, Penguin African Library, Baltimore, Maryland, Penguin, 1963.

The Word is Here: Poetry from Modern Africa, ed. Keoropetse Kgositsile, Garden City, N.Y., Anchor Books, Doubleday, 1973.

Black Orpheus, No. 15, Ibadan, Nigeria, August, 1964.
African Writing Today, ed. Ezekiel Mphahlele, London, Penguin, 1963.
When Bullets Begin to Flower, ed. Margaret Dickenson, Nairobi, East Africa Publishing House, 1972.

Neto, Agostinho — Critical Studies
Davidson, Basil, Preface to *Sagrada Esperança,* pp. 1-6.
Holness, Marga, Introduction to *Sagrada Esperança,* pp. 7-33.
Merwin, W.S., "Agostinho Neto" in *Introduction to African Literature,* Ulli Beier, ed., Evanston, Northwestern University Press, 1967.

Bessa Victor, Geraldo
A Poesia e a Política. Luanda, 1937. (Essays)
Ecos Dispersos. Lisbon, 1941. (Poetry)
Ao Som das Marimbas. Lisbon, Livraria Portugália, 1943. (Poetry)
Debaixo do Ceu. Lisbon, Editorial Império, 1949. (Poetry)
Minha Terra e Minha Dama. Lisbon, 1952. (Essays)
Cubata Abandonada. Lisbon, Agência-Geral do Ultramar, 1958, 2nd. ed., Braga, Editora Pax, 1966. (Poetry)
Mucanda. Braga, Editora Pax, 1964; 2nd edition, 1965. (Poetry)
Sanzala sem Batuque. Braga, Editora Pax, 1967. (Short Stories)
Quinjango no Folclore Angolense. Braga, Editora Pax, 1970. (Essay)
Debaixo de Ceu, Mucanda, Cubata Abandonada. Nendeln, Liechtenstein, Kraus Reprint, 1970. (Poetry)
Ao som das Marimbas, Poèmes Africains. Nendeln, Liechtenstein, Kraus Reprint, 1973. (poetry)
"Problemática da Cultura Angolana." Lisbon, *Boletim da Sociedade de Geografia de Lisboa,* Jan.-March-April, June, 1973. (Essay)
Monandengue, Lisbon, Livraria Portugal, 1973. (Poetry)
Ensaio Crítico Sobre A Primeira Colecção de Proverbias Angolenses. Lisbon, Editorial Enciclopédia, Lda., 1975. (Essay)
Intelectuais Angolenses dos Seculos XIX e XX — Fascículo I: Augusto Bastos, Lisbon, 1975. (Essay)

Bessa Victor, Geraldo — Individual Poems Appear In:
Poèmes Africains. French translations by Gaston-Henry Aufrère of twenty-nine selected poems.
Reistência Africana.
No Reino de Caliban, Vol. II.
Antologia de Poesia Negra de Expressão Portuguesa.
Poetas Angolanos.
Angola, O Ultramar Portugues, no. 10, ed. Luis Ferjaz Trigueiros, Lisbon, Livaria Bertrand, 1961(?).
Okike. English translations of selected poems by Donald Burness, Vol. VI, Winter, 1974.

SELECTED BIBLIOGRAPHY

Ba Shiru. English translations of selected poems by Donald Burness, Vol. VI, Fall, 1974.

Bessa Victor, Geraldo — Critical Studies

Aufrère, Gaston-Henry, Preface to *Poèmes Africains,* pp. 7-10.

Brambilla, Christina, Study of *Sanzala sem Batuque* in *Nigrizia,* Verona, Italy (other details not known).

Burness, Donald, "The Short Stories of Geraldo Bessa Victor," *Ba Shiru,* Vol. VI, Fall, 1974.

Dória, A. Alvaro, "Um Poeta da Negritude," Guimaraes, 1966; reprint from *Gil Vicente,* August, 1966.

António, Mário

Poesias. Lisbon, 1965. (Poetry)

Amor. Lisbon, Casa dos Estudantes do Império, 1960. (Poetry)

Poemas e Canto Miúdo. Sá da Bandeira, Publicações Imbondeiro, 1961. (Poetry)

A Sociedade Angolana do Fim do Século XIX e um Seu Escritor. Luanda, Editorial Nós, 1961. (Essay)

Gente Para Romance: Alvaro, Lígia, António. Colecção Imbondeiro, 19, Sá da Bandeira, Imbondeiro, 1961. (Short Stories)

Chingufo-Poemas Angolanos. Lisbon, Agência Geral do Ultramar, 1962. (Poetry)

Poesia Angolana de Tomaz Vieira da Cruz. Preface and Anthology, Lisbon, Casa dos Estudantes do Império, 1963. (Essay)

100 Poemas. Luanda, ABC, 1963. (Poetry)

Crónica da Cidade Estranha. Lisbon, Agência Geral do Ultramar, 1964. (Short Stories)

Farra no Fim de Semana. Braga, Editora Pax, 1965. (Short Stories)

Era, Tempo de Poesia. Sá da Bandeira, Publicações Imbondeiro, 1966. (Poetry)

Mahezu-Tradições Angolanas. Lisbon, Procuradoria dos Estudantes Ultramarinos, 1966. (Short Stories)

Rosto de Europa. Colecção Metropole e Ultramar, 40, Braga, Editora Pax, 1968. (Poetry)

Nossa Senhora da Vitória de Massangano. Luanda, 1968. (Poetry)

"Notas de Viagem" and "Pérgamo II" — poems in *Boletim Cultural da Câmara Municipal de Luanda,* no. 44, July-Aug.-Sept., 1974.

"Cipaio" in *Mensagem,* Luanda, 1951. (Short Story)

"O Cozinhiero Vicente" (Short Story), in *Contistas Angolanos,* edited by Fernando Mourão, Lisbon, Casa dos Estudantes do Imperio, 1960. (Story)

Introduction to *Poetas Angolanos,* ed. Carlos Eduardo, Lisbon, Casa dos Estudantes do Império, 1959. (Essay)

Para a Historia do Trabalho em Angola — A Escravatura Luandense no Terceiro Quartel de Seculo XIX — 1963. (Essay)

"Aspectos Sociais de Luanda Inferidos dos Anuncios Publicados na Sua Imprensa — Análise Preliminar ao Ano de 1851." Conference, V Colóquio Internacional de Estudos Luso-Brasilieros, Coimbra, 1965. (Essay)

"Colaborações Angolanas no Almanach de Lembranças, 1851-1900" in *Boletim do Instituto de Investigação Cientifica de Angola,* III, 1966. (Essay)

"Influências da Literatura Brasileira sobre as Literaturas Português do Atlántico Tropical." Conference, Lisbon, 1967, mimeographed. (Essay)

"Francisco Tenreiro, poeta." Introduction to *Obra Poética* of Tenreiro, Lisbon, 1967. (Essay)

"Situação da Literatura no 'Espaço Portuguese'." Conference, Lisbon, 1967, mimeographed. (Essay)

Luanda, "Ilha" Crioula. Lisbon, Agência-Geral do Ultramar, 1968. (Five essays, including studies on Assis Junior, Tomaz Vieira da Cruz and Oscar Ribas)

"Unidade e Diferenciação Linguisticas na Literatura Ultramarina Portuguesa." Lisbon, Sociedad de Geografia, Jan-March, 1968, pp. 17-33 (Essay)

O Primeiro Livro de Poemas Publicado na África Portuguesa. Separata da Revista 'Ocidente' — Vol. LXXIX, Lisbon, 1970. (Essay)

"African Writers in Portuguese." *African Arts,* III, 2, Los Angeles, Winter, 1970. (Essay)

"Para Uma Perspectiva Crioula da Literatura Angolana." Cadernos 'Gil Vicente' Guimarães, 1974. (Essay)

"Inquerito: O Futuro de Português Como Lingua Literaria em Africa." *Colóquio,* no. 21, Sept., 1974, pp. 14-15. (Essay)

António, Mário — Individual Poems Appear In:
Reistência Africana.
No Reino de Caliban, Vol. II.
Antologia de Poesia Negra de Expressão Portuguesa.
Poetas Angolanos.
Angola.
New Sum of Poetry from the Negro World.
Présence Africaine, no. 57, First Trimester, 1966.

António, Mário — Critical Studies
Magarido, Alfredo, "A Poesia de Mário António" in *100 Poems,* (first in *Diario de Lisboa,* Oct. 10 and 17, 1960).

Lopes, Baltasar (Pseudonym—Osvaldo Alcântara)
"João que Mameu na Burra." 1940. (Short Story)
Chiquinho. São Vicente, Claridade, 1947. (Novel)
    2nd edition — *Colecção Autores Portugueses,* 2, Lisbon, Prelo, 1961.
    3rd edition — Lisbon, Prelo, 1970.
Cabo Verde Visto por Gilberto Freire. Praia, 1956. (Essay)

Editor, *Antologia da Ficção Cabo-Verdiana Contemporânea,* Praia (Cape Verde) Imprensa Nacional, 1960. (Also included are six of Lopes' short stories, two chapter excerpts from *Chiquinho* and "A Caderneta," "Balanguinho," "Dona Mana" and "Muminha Vai Para a Escola.")

Introduction to *A Aventura Crioula* by Manuel Ferreira, *Colecção Temas Portugueses,* Lisbon, Plátano Editora, S.A.R.L., 1973. (Essay)

Lopes, Baltasar — Individual Poems Appear In:

Claridade no. 2, 1936; no. 5, 1947; no. 6, 1948; no 7, 1949; no 8, 1958; *Colóquio,* no. 14, 1973.

No Reino De Caliban. Lisbon, Seara Nova, 1975. Vol. I.

Antologia de Poesia Negra de Expressão Portuguesa.

Poesia de Cabo Verde, Lisbon, 1944.

Cabo Verde, Guiné, S. Tomé e Príncipe, Marcau e Timor. Antologia da Terra Portuguesa no. 16, ed. Luís Ferjaz Trigueiros, Lisbon, Livraria Bertrand, 1963(?).

Modernos Poetas Cabo-Verdianos, Praia, 1961.

Poetas e Contistas Africanos, São Paulo, 1963.

Literatura Africana de Expressão Portuguesa, Vol. I, Poesia, Argel, 1967.

Lopes, Baltasar — Selected Prose Appears In:

Literatura Africana de Expressão Portuguesa, Vol. 2, Prosa, Argel, 1968.

Contos Portugueses de Ultramar, Vol. 1, Porto, 1969.

Antologia do Conto Ultramarino, ed. Amândio César, Lisbon, Editorial Verbo, 1972.

Lopes, Baltasar — Critical Studies

Araujo, Norman, *A Study of Cape Verdean Literature,* Boston, Boston College, 1966.

Ferreira, Manuel, *A Aventura Crioula,* pp. 105-111, 151-154, and many others.

Figueiredo, Jaime de, essay on "Nocturno" of Osvaldo Alcântara, Praia, 1956 (reprint from *Cabo Verde,* no. 49).

Gonçalves, António Aurélio, "Problemas da Literatura Romanesca em Cabo Verde," in *Antologia de Ficção Cabo-Verdiana Contemporânea.*

Honwana, Luís Bernardo

Nós Matámos o Cão-Tinhoso. Lourenço Marques, Publicações Tribuna, 1964. (Short Stories)
    2nd edition — Porto, Afontamento, 1972.
    3rd edition — in Mozambique, 1975(?).
English translation, *We Killed Mangy Dog,* by Dorothy Guedes, African Writers Series, no. 60, London, Heinemann, 1969.

Honwana, Luís Bernardo — Individual Stories Appear In:

Antologia do Conto Ultramarino, ed. Amândio César. Lisbon, Editorial Verbo, 1972.

African Writing Today. Political Spider and Other Stories, ed. Ulli Beier. African Writers Series, no. 58, London, Heinemann, 1969.

Modern African Prose, ed. Richard Rive, African Writers Series, no. 9, London, Heinemann, 1964.

General Studies on Lusophone African Literature

Burness, Donald. "Lusophone African Literature." paper presented at Translation '74. Columbia University. New York, N.Y., Dec. 1974.

Burness, Donald. "Angolan Writing: an Arm of Liberation." paper presented at African Literature Association meeting, U. of Wisconsin, March, 1977.

Burness, Donald. "L'Optimisme dans la Littérature de l'Angola." paper presented at 7e Colloque de l'Association Canadienne des Etudes Africaines, U. of Sherbrooke, Québec, Canada. May, 1977.

César (Pires Monteiro), Amândio. *Parágafos de Literatura Ultramarina.* Lisbon, Sociedade de Expansão Cultural, 1967.

Dathorne, O.R. *The Black Mind: A History of African Literature.* Minneapolis, Univ. of Minnesota Press, 1974.

Hamilton, Russell. *Vocies from an Empire.* Minneapolis, University of Minnesota Press, 1975.

Klima, Vladimir and Ortova Jarmili. *Moderní Literatury Subsharské Afriky.* Prague, Universita 17 Listopadu V, 1971, pp. 110-132.

Moser, Gerald. *Essays in Portuguese-African Literature.* Pennsylvania State Studies no. 26, University Park, Penn., Administrative Committee on Research — The Pennsylvania State University, 1969.

Preto-Rodas, Richard. *Negritude as a Theme in the Poetry of the Portuguese-Speaking World.* Humanities Monographs Ser. No. 31. University Press of Florida, 1970.

Riausova, Elena. *As Literaturas da Africa de Expressão Portuguesa.* Moscow, ed. Nauka, 1973.

INDEX

Abrahams, Peter, 46
Achebe, Chinua, xiv, 8, 51, 73
"Adeus a Hora da Largada" (Neto), 24
African Writers Series, xi
African Writing Today (Mphahlele), 97
Albuquerque, Orlando de, 104
Alcântara, Osvaldo (pseudonym for Baltasar Lopes, the poet), 76
Aljube prison, 30
"Alturas de Macchu Picchu, Las" (Neruda), 14
Amade, Jorge, 2, 4, 76
"Amer Sobre a Marca da Negritude" (Bessa Victor), 41
Andrade, Costa, xiv, 33
Andrade, Mário de, xii, xiii, xiv, xvi, xvii, 4
Antologia da Ficção Cabe-Verdiana Contemperânea (Lopes), 91, 92
Antologia de Poesia Negra de Expressão Portuguesa (Mário de Andrade), xii, xvi
António, Mário, xiv, xvi, xvii, 2, 55-73
Ao Som das Marimbas (Bessa Victor), 35
"Apontamento na Quitanda do Muceque" (Bessa Victor), 36, 38, 45, 46
Armah, Ayi Kwei, 70
"Assim Clamava Esgotado" (Neto), 32
Assis Junior, 48
Atlântico, 76
Aufrère, Gaston-Henry, 35
"Avó Maria" (António), 66-68
"Avó Negra" (António), 56, 58-59, 64

Awoonor, Kofi, xiv, 51
"Balanguinho" (Lopes), 92
Barbosa, Jorge, 76, 80, 85, 91, 95
Ba Shiru, 35
Bastide, Roger, 49
Beier, Ulli, 97
Benenson, Peter, 20
Beside the Fire (Eligwe), 13
Bessa Victor, Geraldo, xvi, xvii, 35-54
Black Orpheus, 97
Black Skin, White Masks (Fanon), 47
Boletim Cabo Verde, 92
"Bouquet de Rosas para ti, um" (Neto), 27-28
"Braile" (António), 63
Brazilian modernists, xvi, 2, 76
Brutus, Dennis, 7

Cabo Verde, 76
Cabo-verdianidade, xvi, 76
"Caderneta, A" (Lopes), 92-93
Caetano, Marcelo, xi, 1, 31
Camões, Luís de, 2
Cardoso, Lopes, 70
Cardoso, Pedro, 1
"Carnival" (Bessa Victor), 49, 52-53
Casa dos Estudantes do Império, 7, 20
Castro Francina, Manuel Alves de, xiv
Caxias prison, 19
Cazumbi (Vieira da Cruz), 38

145

INDEX

Césaire, Aimé, 75
"Chaka" (Senghor), 80
Chatelian, Heli, xiv, 70
Chingufo-Poemas Angolanos (António), 55
Chiquinho (Lopes), 81-92
"Chuva' (Antonio), 60
"*Chuva Braba* (Manual Lopes), 92
Cidade e a Infância, A (Vieira), 16
Claridade, 76, 79, 91, 92, 94
"Colonialist Criticism" (Achebe), 73
Colóquio, 76
"Comboio e o Navio, O" (Bessa Victor), 49-50
"Consciencialização na Literatura Caboverdiana" (Silveira), 94
Contistas Angolanas (Mourão), 26
Contos Populares de Angola (Chatelian), 70
Costa, Orlanda da, 8
"Cozinheiro Vincente, O" (António), 65
Craveirinha, José, xiv
"Crianças" (Bessa Victor, 39
"Criar" (Neto), 33
Crioulo language in Cape Verde, xvi, 76
Crónica da Cidade Estranha (António), 68-70
Cubata Abandonada, (Bessa Victor), 35, 40
Cultura, 2
"Cultura Negro-Africana e Assimilação" (Mário de Andrade), xii

Dachau, 7
Davidson, Basil, 20
Debaixo do Céu (Bessa Victor), 35
"Depressa" (Neto), 30
Dias, João, 104
"Dina" (Honwana), 97, 100-101
"Do Amor Impossivel" (António), 60
"Dois Poemas do Mar" (Franca), 80
"Domingas ou as Duas Faces da Alma" (Bessa Victor), 47-52
"Dona Mana" (Lopes), 92
Dória, Alvaro, 45
Dramouss (Laye), 53
Duarte, Pedro, 95
'Duelo de Gigantes" (Bessa Victor), 47

Ecos Dispersos (Bessa Victor), 35
Eduardo, Carlos, 56
Eligwe, Obioma, 13
Enfant Noir, L' (Laye), 81, 84

Ensaio Crítico Sobre a Primeira Colecção de Provérbios Angolenses (Bessa Victor), 35
"Enterro de Nhâ Candinha Sena, O" (Gonçalves),
"E Proibido Brincar" (Bessa Victor), 46-47
Era, Tempo de Poesia (António), 55
Ervedosa, Carlos, 8
"Esperando a Noite" (Bessa Victor), 40
"Estória da Galinha e do Ovo" (Vieira), 12-14
"Estória do Ladrao e do Papagaio" (Vieira), 11-12, 15
L'Etudiant Noir, 2
"Evora" (António), 62-63

"Fado" (António), 63-64
Fanon, Franz, 47
Farra no Fim de Semana (António), 66-68
"Feitiço no Bufo Toneto, O" (Vieira), 9-11
Ferreira, Manuel, 75
"Filha de Ngana Chica, A" (Bessa Victor), 47, 48
"Fogo e Ritmo" (Neto), 34
Fonseca, Lília da, 8
Franca, Arnaldo, 80
Freyre, Gilberto, xii
Fugard, Athol, 7

Ginga, Queen, xviii, 31
"Godido" (Dias), 104
Gomes, General Costa, 31
Gonçalves, António Aurélio, xvi, 92, 95
Guedes, Dorthy, 97
Guillén, Nicolás, 19
Gulag Archipelago, 7
Gulbenkian Foundation, 55

"Havemos de Voltar" (Neto), 28-30, 33
Heinemann, xi, 97
"Historia Triste, A" (António), 59
Homecoming (Ngugi), 6
Honwana, Luís Bernardo, xiv, xvi, xvii, 97-105

Igbo language, xiv
Intelectuais Angolenses dos Séculos XIX e XX (Bessa Victor), 35
International Amnesty, 20
Island, The (Fugard), 7

Jacinto, António, xii, xiii, xiv, xvi, xvii, 1, 2, 32, 38

Jacinto, Tomás, 2, 33

Kalunga, 26
Kane, Cheikh Hamidou, 51
Kiluanji, Ngola, 31
Kimbundu language, xiv, 2, 26, 32, 45, 48, 59, 67, 70
Knopfli, Rui, 38

"Lago" (António), 72
Lara, Alda, 2
Laye, Camara, 51, 53, 84
Lessa, Almerindo, xviii
Lessing, Doris, 20
Letters to Martha (Brutus), 7
Lewis, C. Day, 20
Lima, Jorge de, 76
Lima, Manuel dos Santos, xiv
Lopes, Baltasar, xiv, xvi, xvii, 75-95, 97
Lopes, Francisco, 95
Lopes, Manuel, 76, 80, 92, 95
Luuanda (Vieira), 2, 11-14, 68

Machel, Samora, xiv, 104
Mahezu (António), 70-72
"Mamãe" (Lopes), 76
"Mãos dos Pretos, As" (Honwana), 97, 103-104
"Mãos Esculturais" (Neto), 27
"Mar" (Lopes), 78, 80
Mariano, Gabriel, 95
Martins, Ovídio, 45
"Meia-noite na Quitanda" (Neto), 24
"Menino Negro não Entrou na Roda, O" (Bessa Victor), 38-39
Mensagem, 2, 55, 76
Mingas, Ruy, 33
Modern African Prose (Rive), 97
Monandengue (Bessa Victor), 35, 36, 43
Morna, 85, 91, 94-95
Moser, Gerald, xiii, xvii
Mourão, Fernando, 26
Mphahlele, Ezekiel, 97
M.P.L.A. (Popular Movement for the Liberation of Angola), xiv, 1, 20, 31, 38
Mucanda (Bessa Victor), 35, 36, 40
"Muminha Vai para a Escola" (Lopes), 92
Murdock, Iris, 20
"Mussunda Amigo" (Neto), 25

"Na Hora da Independência de Angola" (Bessa Victor), 44
"Na Noite de Batuque" (Bessa Victor), 40
"Não Invoquei o Sonho para Amar-te" (António), 61
"Naufrágio" (Manuel Lopes), 80
"Nausea" (Neto), 26
Negritude poetry of Portuguese expression, xiii, xvi, 20, 33, 35, 36, 45; of French expression, 20, 45
"Negro Vagabundo, O" (Bessa Victor), 42, 43
Neruda, Pablo, 14
Neto, Agostinho, xi, xiv, xvi, xvii, 2, 19-34
Ngugi, James, 6
"Nhinguitimo" (Honwana), 100-101
No Antigamente na Vida (Vieira), xvi, 16-17
"Noite" (Neto), 22-23
Nós Matamos o Cão-Tinhoso (We Killed Mangy Dog), (Honwana), 97-105
Nós, os do Makulusu (Vieira), 2, 14-16
Nossa Senhora da Vitória de Massangano (Antonio), 55
Nzinga Mbandi (Pacavira), xviii

Okara, Gabriel, 45
Okigbo, Christopher, 45
Okike, 35
Oliveira, Osório de, xviii, 95
Osborne, John, 20
Oyono, Ferdinand, 2

Pacavira, Manuel, xviii
"Papá, Cobra e Eu" (Honwana), 97, 101-103
"Partida para o Contrato" (Neto), 22
"Passeio de Barco" (António), 70
"Pequeno, um Grande Chefe, Um" (António), 71-72
Persecution (Benenson), 20
Pessoa, Fernando, 76
Peters, Lenrie, 70
PIDE (Portuguese Secret Police), 7
Pires, Virgílio Avelino
"Poema da Fraternidade Frustrada" (Bessa Victor), 42
"Poemas do Mar" (Barbosa), 80
Poemas e Canto Miúdo (António), 35
Poesias (António), 55
Poetas Angolanos (Eduardo), 56
Poetry of Combat Prize, 20
Political Spider and Other Stories (Beier), 97

INDEX

"Praga, A" (Ribas), 10
Presença, 76
"Presença" (Lopes), 78, 80
"Procura de um Poema, A" (António), 60
"Pródiga" (Gonçalves), 92
Proust, Marcel, 68
Provincia de Angola, A, 44

Quinjango no Folclore Angolense (Bessa Victor), 48
Quissange (Vieira da Cruz), 38
"Quitandeira" (Neto), 23, 27

"Reconquista, A" (Neto), 27
Rego, José Lins de, 76
"Rei Destronado" (Bessa Victor), 53
Ribas, Oscar, xviii, 10, 48
Rive, Richard, 97
Rivera, Diego, 19
Robben Island, 7
Robben Island (Zwelonke), 7
Rodrigues, Urbana Tavares, 8

"Sábado nos Musseques" (Neto), 24
Sagrada Esperança (Neto), 20-34
Salazar, xi
Salema, Alvaro, 45
Santos, Arnaldo, 2
Santos, Marcelino dos, xvii
Sanzala sem Batuque (Bessa Victor), 35, 46-53
Sartre, Jean-Paul, 19
Saudade (in Bessa Victor's stories), 49-53
Second Round, The (Peters), 70
Sembène, Ousmane, 51
Senghor, Léopold Sédar, xiii, 20, 22, 45, 76, 80
Shaka Zulu, 67
Sillitoe, Allan, 20
Silveira, Onésimo, 94

"Sinfonia" (Neto), 32
"Sombros" (Neto), 24
Soromenho, Castro, xiii, xvii, xviii, 18, 38
Sousa, Noémia de, 8
Souza e Oliveira, Dr. Saturnino de, xiv
Soyinka, Wole, 45, 51
Symbolist poetry, 62

Tarrafal prison, 1, 14
Tatuagem (Vieira da Cruz), 38
Tavares, Eugénio, xvi, 94
Tenreiro, Francisco, xvi
"Terra Longismo", 81, 90
Terra Morta (Soromenho), xviii, 18
Things Fall Apart (Achebe), 8, 81
"Thoughts on the African Novel" (Achebe), 73
Tiberghien, Chantal, 4
Tutuola, Amos, 71

Valéry, Paul, 66
"Vavó Xixi e seu Neto Zeca Santos" (Vieira), 11-12
Velhas Estorias (Vieira), 11
"Velha Mulemba, A" (Bessa Victor), 41-42
"Velha Mulher, A" (Honwana), 105
"Verde das Palmeiras da Minha Mocidade, O" (Neto), 28
Veríssimo, Erico, 76
Vértice, 76, 92
Vidas Novas (Vieira), 7-11
Vida Verdadeira de Domingos Xavier, A (Vieira), 1, 4-7, 8, 9
Vieira, Luandino, xi, xiii, xiv, xvi, 1-17, 55, 65, 97
Vieira de Cruz, Tomaz, 38
"Voz Igual, A" (Neto), 31

Wilson, Angus, 20

Zwelonke, Z.M., 7